ALA Editions • **SPECIAL REPORTS**

INTRODUCING RDA

A GUIDE TO THE BASICS

CHRIS OLIVER

AMERICAN LIBRARY ASSOCIATION

Chicago   2010

Chris Oliver supervises cataloging at the McGill University Library. She is a member of the Canadian Library Association and has chaired the Canadian Committee on Cataloguing.

Printed in the United States of America

14   13   5   4

While extensive effort has gone into ensuring the reliability of the information in this book, the publisher makes no warranty, express or implied, with respect to the material contained herein.

ISBN: 978-0-8389-3594-1

Library of Congress Cataloging-in-Publication Data
Oliver, Christine Tomaszuk.
　　Introducing RDA : a guide to the basics / Chris Oliver.
　　　　p.　　cm.
　　Includes bibliographical references and index.
　　ISBN 978-0-8389-3594-1 (alk. paper)
　　1. Resource description & access. 2. Descriptive cataloging—Standards. I. Title.
　　Z694.15.R47O45 2010
　　025.3'2—dc22

2010021719

Series cover design by Casey Bayer. Series text design in Palatino Linotype and Avenir by Karen Sheets de Gracia. Composition by Dianne M. Rooney.

∞ This paper meets the requirements of ANSI/NISO Z39.48-1992 (Permanence of Paper).

ALA Editions also publishes its books in a variety of electronic formats. For more information, visit the ALA Store at www.alastore.ala.org and select eEditions.

CONTENTS

ACKNOWLEDGMENTS

I would like to acknowledge those who generously offered advice and comments. With much appreciation, thank you to Tom Delsey, Dr. Barbara Tillett, Margaret Stewart, Pat Riva, Nanette Naught, Mary Curran, Marc Richard, and Nevenka Koscevic.

ABBREVIATIONS

CoP	Committee of Principals
AACR	Anglo-American Cataloguing Rules
AACR2	Anglo-American Cataloguing Rules, 2nd edition
FRAD	Functional Requirements for Authority Data
FRSAD	Functional Requirements for Subject Authority Data
FRBR	Functional Requirements for Bibliographic Records
IFLA	International Federation of Library Associations and Institutions
ISBD	International Standard Bibliographic Description
JSC	Joint Steering Committee
MARC 21	MARC = MAchine Readable Cataloging MARC 21 = harmonization of USMARC and CAN/MARC
MODS	Metadata Object Description Schema
ONIX	ONline Information eXchange
RDA	Resource Description and Access

1

WHAT IS RDA?

RDA, Resource Description and Access, is the new cataloging standard that replaces the Anglo-American Cataloguing Rules, 2nd edition (AACR2). Though it has strong links to AACR2, RDA is quite different because it is based on a theoretical framework, it is designed for the digital environment, and it has a broader scope than AACR2.

BASED ON A THEORETICAL FRAMEWORK

Like AACR, RDA consists of a set of practical instructions. However, RDA is based on a theoretical framework that defines the shape, structure, and content of the new standard. The key to understanding RDA is its alignment with the two conceptual models, Functional Requirements for Bibliographic Records (FRBR) and Functional Requirements for Authority Data (FRAD).[1] FRAD is an extension of the FRBR model. The models are a way of understanding the bibliographic universe. They identify the tasks that users need to accomplish during the process of resource discovery and demonstrate how different types of bibliographic and authority data support the successful accomplishment of these tasks. FRBR and FRAD provide a theoretical and logically coherent basis on which to build an improved resource-discovery experience for the user.

The opening words of RDA state the overall purpose and scope as providing "a set of guidelines and instructions on formulating data to support resource discovery" (0.0). The phrase "to support resource discovery" conveys a key message about the nature of RDA: this is a standard designed to focus attention on the user and on the tasks that the user carries out in the process of resource discovery. The purpose of recording data is to support the user tasks.

Every instruction in RDA relates back to the user and to the tasks that the user wishes to accomplish. These user tasks have their origin in the FRBR and FRAD models, and are introduced immediately, at the very beginning of RDA (0.0):

Tasks That Use Bibliographic Data	Tasks That Use Authority Data
find	find
identify	identify
select	clarify
obtain	understand

RDA takes as its starting point the theoretical framework expressed in the FRBR and FRAD models. This theoretical framework constitutes a new way of thinking about bibliographic and authority data. This change in approach is reflected throughout the standard, in the organization and structure of the instructions and in the content of the instructions.

DESIGNED FOR THE DIGITAL ENVIRONMENT

The changes in the cataloging environment between the 1960s and 2000s have been enormous, not only because of the rapid proliferation of new types of publications, new forms of content, and new carriers for content, but also because the move into a networked online environment has qualitatively changed the way the library and its users go about their work. RDA is a standard designed for the digital environment.

RDA's purpose is to support the production of robust, or "well-formed," [2] data that can be managed using both current technologies and newly emerging database structures and technologies of the future. RDA is a "content" standard. RDA answers the question, What data should I record and how should I record it? RDA defines the elements required for description and access and gives instructions on formulating the data that is recorded in each element. Data is parsed or segmented into clearly defined elements. The elements may seem choppy after the paragraph style of the ISBDs,[3] but each element is unambiguously defined and contains one particular kind of data. This way of recording data in a set of elements means that RDA is not tied to a single encoding schema or presentation style. RDA data can be encoded using existing schema, such as MARC 21, Dublin Core, MODS,[4] and can also be mapped to other schema, current or future ones. At first release, RDA data can be encoded, stored, and transmitted using existing technology and databases, as MARC records in traditional library catalogs. However, RDA data is also designed for use in the networked environment of the Web and in new types of database structures. RDA data can be used as the basis for a metadata element set that makes data visible and usable in a Web environment.

RDA can be used for the description of both traditional and nontraditional resources, analog and digital, within and beyond the library. A key feature of RDA is the way it is designed to "provide a consistent, flexible, and extensible framework for both the technical and content description of all types of resources and all types of content."[5] It provides the principles and instructions to record data about resources that are currently known and resources that have yet to be developed. A major stumbling block for AACR2 was the description of new types of resources. AACR was originally developed as a cataloging code for print books and journals and other paper-based documents. Although rules for other media were grafted into the code, there was never a cohesive and logically consistent approach to the description of content, media, and carrier. This limitation made it difficult to extend AACR2 rules for the description of new types of resources, notably electronic resources. RDA provides an extensible framework for the description of all types of resources.

For the cataloging community, RDA marks a significant change because it is a standard designed to be used as a Web tool. The standard is delivered primarily as a Web document, within the RDA Toolkit.[6] The content of RDA can be accessed in many ways, to suit different learning styles and different requirements. Some catalogers may choose to start by browsing RDA's table of contents because it provides a good sense of the intellectual organization of the standard and the way in which it is aligned with the FRBR and FRAD conceptual models. Others may prefer to start with the entity relationship diagram (ERD) that gives a visual outline of RDA's content. Others may want to start with one of the practical procedure documents, called workflows. Workflows focus on the instructions that relate to one specific procedure. The Toolkit also includes mappings that indicate how to encode RDA elements with different encoding schema. The workflows and mappings are tools that guide the cataloger in the application of the standard. Libraries can also share workflows and mappings, and customize them, incorporating their local policies and procedures and storing them as part of the Toolkit. The Toolkit includes multiple ways to access and use the instructions and includes tools that support the efficient integration of RDA into daily work. The Toolkit aims to support an efficient implementation of RDA.

EXPANDED SCOPE

RDA is not just for libraries. RDA was designed by the library community for its use, but one of the goals was that RDA should also "be capable of adaptation to meet the specific needs of other communities."[7] One of the features noted above was the flexible and extensible framework that allows for the description of all types of resources, whether traditional library resources, or resources from other cultural heritage communities, such as archives, museums, or digital repositories. The possibility of using RDA in a broader range of contexts is also evident in its definition as a "content" standard, and its adaptability for use in an international context.

Though it comes out of the library milieu, RDA was designed with an awareness of other metadata communities and their resource description standards—communities such as archives, museums, and publishers. The boundaries between metadata communities are meaningless to a user who searches a networked, online environment. By making RDA a content standard, it is possible for other metadata communities to consider using or overlapping with RDA. Data can be stored and transmitted using a variety of encoding schema, including schemas in use within other metadata communities. Likewise, by staying away from instructions about the presentation of the data, the door is opened to a potentially wider community of users, using RDA elements in new and different applications. The greater the compatibility of data between metadata communities, the greater the benefits for the user.

RDA was designed for use in an international context. RDA is the product of international cooperation between the four author countries: Australia, Canada, Great Britain, and the United States. However, "use in an international context" means the potential to be used by many countries around the world, not just by the four author countries. RDA purposely sheds the Anglo-American perspective of AACR. Instructions have been adjusted so that they can be applied by communities that use different languages, scripts, numbering systems, calendars, or measurement units. Also, during the development process, the Joint Steering Committee for Development of RDA, the body responsible for the content of the standard, invited comments from international organizations and the national libraries and national cataloging committees of other countries, countries that use AACR2 and also countries that have their own national cataloging codes. This dialogue at the international level has contributed to achieving the goal of making RDA usable in an international context.

RELATIONSHIP TO AACR2

There are significant differences between RDA and AACR2, but important links between the two standards remain. RDA builds on the foundation of AACR. Many RDA instructions are derived from AACR2. There was also a conscious effort to maintain compatibility with the legacy data of AACR2 records. RDA data can be encoded with the same MARC 21 standard used for AACR2 records. In the early years of RDA implementation, RDA records will be stored and searched in databases and catalogs that are still predominantly composed of AACR2 records.

Much of what makes RDA new and different are the parts that gear it to function effectively within the digital environment, but, at the same time, there is a constant awareness that the standard must also function as a bridge between the past and future environments, and that not all libraries will progress at the same pace into new environments.

IMPACT

RDA is a key step in the improvement of resource discovery because it guides the recording of data. The production of well-formed data is a vital piece of the infrastructure to support search engines and data displays. RDA data alone will not improve navigation and display because the data must be used appropriately by well-designed search engines and search interfaces. Nevertheless, the recording of clear, unambiguous data is a required step in the improvement of resource discovery.

RDA is designed to produce data that can be stored, searched, and retrieved in traditional catalogs. RDA data is also designed for use in the Web environment and with newly emerging database technologies. It positions the library community to take advantage of the networked online environment, and to make library data widely visible, discoverable, and usable.

Implementing RDA will have an immediate impact on catalogers, as well as on library system designers and administrators. Increasingly, as the volume of RDA data grows, it will have an impact on those who use bibliographic and authority data in library catalogs and then in applications on the Web. This book aims to describe some of the basic features of the standard to help with implementation planning and preparation.

NOTES

1. IFLA Study Group on the Functional Requirements for Bibliographic Records, *Functional Requirements for Bibliographic Records: Final Report* (Munich: Saur, 1998). Also online: www.ifla.org/en/publications/functional-requirements-for-bibliographic-records/. IFLA Working Group on Functional Requirements and Numbering of Authority Records (FRANAR), *Functional Requirements for Authority Data: A Conceptual Model* (Munich: Saur, 2009).

2. Well-formed data: "well-formed, i.e., instructions are provided on how to record the values of elements, controlled vocabularies are used where appropriate, and the overall structure is governed by a formal model." Joint Steering Committee for Development of RDA, "RDA Scope and Structure" (JSC/RDA/Scope/Rev/4; July 1, 2009), www.rda-jsc.org/docs/5rda-scoperev4.pdf.

3. International Standard Bibliographic Description: a standard developed under the auspices of the International Federation of Library Associations and Institutions (IFLA) to promote consistency when sharing bibliographic data. See www.ifla.org/en/about-the-isbd-review-group/.

4. For more information about MARC 21, see the MARC Standards website of the Library of Congress, Network Development and MARC Standards Office: www.loc.gov/marc/. For more information about Dublin Core, see the website of the Dublin Core Metadata Initiative: http://dublincore.org. For more information about MODS, the Metadata Object Description Schema, see the MODS website of the Library of Congress Network Development and MARC Standards Office: www.loc.gov/standards/mods/.

5. Joint Steering Committee for Development of RDA, "Strategic Plan for RDA, 2005–2009" (5JSC/Strategic/1/Rev/2; November 1, 2007), www.rda-jsc.org/stratplan.html (last updated: July 1, 2009).

6. RDA Toolkit (Chicago: American Library Association; Ottawa: Canadian Library Association; London: Chartered Institute of Library and Information Professionals [CILIP], 2010–), www.rdatoolkit.org.

7. Ibid.

2

RDA AND THE INTERNATIONAL CONTEXT

RDA AND ITS RELATIONSHIP TO INTERNATIONAL STANDARDS, MODELS, AND PRINCIPLES

For a new standard to be credible and effective, it is important that the new standard align with international standards that are currently in use and share the same understanding of the nature and use of bibliographic data. RDA uses the concepts, vocabulary, and principles that are recognized by the international cataloging community. It builds on existing cataloging traditions while also taking into consideration how library data will be used in the future. Data produced according to RDA instructions can be transmitted, stored, and used with both evolving and existing bibliographic standards. RDA was developed to fit within the grid of international resource description standards.

The 1967 introduction to AACR declares that the rules are based on the Paris Principles, the Statement of Principles adopted by the International Conference on Cataloguing Principles that was held in 1961, in Paris. Conforming to an internationally accepted set of principles lays the groundwork for enabling the exchange of bibliographic data. It is the first step in a process of standardization. Though far from the networked online environment of today, already there was a vision that standardization was an essential step in the goal of universal bibliographic control. In the current environment, we speak of interoperability, resource sharing, and the seamless exchange and reuse of metadata. The scope has become broader but the goal is the same: to break down the barriers that inhibit communication about bibliographic resources. Standardization remains the basic building block.

During the 1970s, with the Paris Principles as a starting point, there were fruitful efforts to develop common ground for bibliographic description at the international level. Through the work of the International Federation of Library Associations and Institutions (IFLA), a descriptive standard was developed and accepted: the International Standard Bibliographic Description (ISBD). The ISBDs were an agreed set of descriptive elements and an agreed convention for the display of bibliographic data. Countries around the world had a common starting point.

The second edition of AACR began by reiterating AACR's alignment with the internationally accepted Paris Principles and also included a statement explaining its conformity with the ISBD framework.

The introduction to RDA continues the AACR practice of situating the standard in relation to existing international standards and initiatives pertaining to bibliographic data. The information given in 0.2 to 0.4 of the introductory chapter explains RDA's relationship to current internationally accepted standards, models, and principles:

0.2 *Relationship to other standards for resource description and access*

0.3 *Conceptual models underlying RDA*

0.4 *Objectives and principles governing resource description and access*

Making these relationships explicit demonstrates that RDA is in step with the international cataloging community.

The statement at 0.2 declares that RDA is built on the foundations of AACR. 0.2 also states that RDA is built on the cataloging traditions on which AACR was based and refers to classic texts such as Cutter's *Rules for a Dictionary Catalog* and Panizzi's "Rules for the Compilation of the Catalogue." RDA brings a new perspective to the activity of cataloging. It introduces new descriptive elements, new approaches to describing content and carrier, new ways to improve access. At the same time, it maintains continuity with the past, building on the cataloging theory embodied in earlier standards. It does not clash with what went before. It enhances and expands previous conventions and standards.

Next in 0.2, there is a list of current resource description standards that have played a role during the development of RDA and with which RDA is compatible:

> Other key standards used in developing RDA include the International Standard Bibliographic Description (ISBD), the MARC 21 Format for Bibliographic Data, and the MARC 21 Format for Authority Data.

> The RDA element set is compatible with ISBD, MARC 21, and Dublin Core. For mappings of the RDA element set to ISBD and MARC 21, see appendices D and E.

> RDA also conforms to the RDA/ONIX Framework for Resource Categorization.

The standards listed in 0.2 are those that currently govern encoding (MARC 21), the presentation of data (ISBD), and some content as well (ISBD and ONIX[1]). For a content standard to function effectively in real world situations, its data must be compatible with existing standards, such as standards that govern encoding or display of data. RDA does not prescribe a particular method of encoding the data, nor a particular style for presenting the data. It limits itself to instructions about the choice of data and how to record it. In its first release, the standard includes detailed mappings between RDA and the MARC 21 encoding schema and between RDA and the presentation format of ISBD. These mappings are in appendices, not in the main body of the standard. By defining the scope of the standard as a content standard, it allows flexibility for the future because RDA can be used with different encoding schema and presentation formats.

The statement at 0.3 identifies one of the defining features of RDA: its alignment with the conceptual models developed under the auspices of IFLA. The FRBR and FRAD models provide the underlying theoretical framework that shapes RDA. The influence of the models is evident in the structure of RDA, in the vocabulary and concepts, and in the emphasis on the user and the tasks the user needs to accomplish. At first, one might question why RDA's relationship with the conceptual models is juxtaposed with its relationship to resource description standards. The models are not resource description standards, but they do define an internationally shared understanding of bibliographic data. Alignment with the conceptual models has had a major effect on the content of RDA, and has also brought RDA into line with a globally recognized consensus about the nature of bibliographic data.

In the ten years since its publication, the FRBR conceptual model has been accepted internationally as a model with valid explanatory power. The FRBR model has its origin in the report of an international study group appointed by IFLA to examine the functional requirements for bibliographic records.[2] The study group developed an entity relationship model as the means to analyze bibliographic records and make their recommendations about a basic level of functionality for records created by national bibliographic agencies. While the recommendations about basic functionality are useful, it is the model itself that has continued to be discussed, applied, and developed. The model has led to a major change in the way bibliographic data is understood. It has also introduced a common vocabulary and understanding of bibliographic data that is shared at an international level.

> FRBR's enduring strength is its neutrality as to bibliographic conventions and its theoretical approach that focuses on the user, the object and function—all of which has enabled its timelessness to application.[3]

> Since the release of FRBR in 1998, there has been a growing reflection in the bibliographic community around the ideas it represents. FRBR has provided a unifying framework and a common terminology for discussion. . . . Since FRBR, most theoretical studies and applications have been using FRBR terminology.[4]

Evidence of the explanatory power of the model can be seen in the volume of writing about FRBR, and the number of projects that take FRBR as their framework. The FRBR bibliography[5] documents how the FRBR model has been received around the world and used as the starting point for new applications, new research, and new cataloging codes.

The FRBR and FRAD conceptual models provide RDA with the vocabulary and concepts of the international cataloging community. RDA 0.4 clearly states the relationship between the IFLA Statement of International Cataloguing Principles[6] and RDA:

> The IFLA Statement of International Cataloguing Principles informs the cataloguing principles used throughout RDA (0.4.1).

The Paris Principles of 1961 were written at the time of the card catalog for a print-based environment. Over a period of five years, from 2003 to 2007, meetings were held under the auspices of IFLA to consult with catalogers on all continents and to produce an updated version of the international cataloging principles. The IFLA Meetings of Experts on an International Cataloguing Code reached consensus on a final version of the statement of principles, which was published in 2009. The International Cataloguing Principles (ICP) and RDA were developed and written over the same period of years. The Joint Steering Committee carefully monitored the development of ICP and kept RDA in step with those principles.

The introduction to the Statement of International Cataloguing Principles shows the relatedness of international initiatives in the area of cataloging and bibliographic data:

> This statement builds on the great cataloguing traditions of the world, and also on the conceptual model in the IFLA *Functional Requirements for Bibliographic Records (FRBR)*.[7]

Thus, alignment with the models and compatibility with the principles keeps RDA consistent with the concepts and understandings shared by the international cataloging community.

To complete the picture of RDA's relationships to international standards, RDA occasionally refers to external vocabulary encoding schemes, such as the list of scripts specified in an ISO (International Organization for Standardization) standard.

> **0.12** *Encoding RDA Data*
>
> . . .
>
> For certain elements, the RDA instructions reference external vocabulary encoding schemes (e.g., the instructions on recording the script or scripts used to express the language content of the resource reference the terms listed in ISO 15924).

> **7.13.2.3** *Recording Scripts*
>
> Record the script or scripts used to express the language content of the resource using one or more of the terms listed in ISO 15924 (http://www.unicode.org/iso15924/codelists.html).

Generally, RDA instructions do not reference external schemes. Whether this practice will be expanded or not will depend on the Joint Steering Committee's assessment of the value of such referencing. Using a standard scheme may facilitate automated processing for retrieval and matching, but the displayed data must be readily recognizable and understandable by the user. Expansion may depend on the functionality of future software to manage encoded data and present useful data displays.

RDA encourages the recording of identifiers. Identifiers from internationally recognized schemes such as ISBN and ISSN continue to be used, as they were in AACR. RDA also expands to accept other recognized identifier schemes.

> **2.15.1**   *Basic Instructions on Recording Identifiers for the Manifestation*
>
> **2.15.1.1**   *Scope*
>
> . . .
>
> Identifiers for manifestations include identifiers registered applying internationally recognized schemes (e.g., ISBN, ISSN, URN), as well as other identifiers assigned by publishers, distributors, government publications agencies, document clearing-houses, archives, etc., following internally devised schemes.

RDA builds on the principles and methods of its predecessor, AACR. It is still deeply influenced by the ISBD framework. The data that is created according to its instructions can be used with existing encoding standards, such as MARC 21, and displayed using recognized conventions, such as an ISBD presentation of data.

RDA uses the concepts, vocabulary, and principles that are recognized and used by the international cataloging community. It leaves open the possibility of using RDA data with newly evolving encoding formats and storing the data in new types of database structures. RDA encourages the formulation of data according to existing international standards, when applicable. RDA does not operate in a vacuum. It fits within the grid of international bibliographic standards, ensuring that the data produced according to RDA is effective and usable.

RDA AND ITS USE IN AN INTERNATIONAL CONTEXT

RDA is a standard that has been developed through a cooperative international process involving the national libraries, national library associations, and national cataloging committees of Australia, Canada, Great Britain, and the United States. AACR was written and revised using the same process. AACR was adopted by the four author countries and went on to be adopted by many countries around the world. AACR was translated into twenty-five languages, attesting to its widespread use outside of Anglophone countries. AACR2 was extensively used around the world, even though it was not designed for such use and implementation was not straightforward for communities that used different languages, scripts, calendars, etc. In 1997, the International Conference on the Principles and Future Development of AACR was held in Toronto. It was hosted by the Joint Steering Committee for Revision of AACR, the body responsible for the content of AACR2. International experts were invited to identify areas for future development. One of these areas was the need to broaden the scope of the standard so that it would be easier to use in various international contexts.

Since the early days of the development process, there has been an effort to internationalize RDA and to make RDA easily applicable by communities around the world. AACR was written from the perspective of the Anglo-American cataloging community. Internationalization has meant reducing the Anglo-American bias and writing the instructions so that they can easily be applied by communities using different languages, scripts, numbering systems, calendars, or measurement units. RDA specifically includes a statement on internationalization, and the scope is clearly stated:

0.11.1 *General*

RDA is designed for use in an international context.

Instructions are given with options to cover the possibility of using different languages, scripts, numbering systems, etc. When the instruction is to record data, rather than transcribe data, RDA instructions will often refer to using the language or script or numerals "preferred by the agency creating the data."

As will be seen in more detail, RDA includes lists of controlled vocabulary in later chapters for use in recording elements such as content type, media type, and carrier type. These lists use English language terms, but the statement on internationalization points out that it is expected that these lists will be translated to suit the cataloging context:

0.11.2 *Language and Script*

. . .

There are, however, a number of instructions that specify the use of an English-language term (e.g., *publisher not identified*) or provide a controlled list of terms in English (e.g., the terms used to designate media type, carrier type, base material). Agencies creating data for use in a different language or script context may modify such instructions to reflect their own language or script preferences and replace the English-language terms specified in RDA with terms appropriate for use in their context. Authorized translations of RDA will do likewise.

Not only was RDA intended for use to describe all types of resources from around the world, it was also intended for use by cataloging communities around the globe.

As part of the development process, the Joint Steering Committee broadened the forum for discussion of RDA content in two ways: first, it made the drafts available to everyone around the world, by posting them on an open website; second, it formally invited comments on the drafts from the national libraries and national cataloging committees of other countries, both current AACR2 users and those that have their own national cataloging codes. Many countries responded, and their comments provided useful feedback during the development process. The intention to internationalize RDA is an ongoing effort and will continue with further changes in future releases. The first release begins to realize this intention.

RDA has the potential to be used by many countries around the world. RDA reflects the International Cataloguing Principles (ICP), and is aligned with the internationally accepted FRBR and FRAD models. RDA is an early example of the application of shared cataloging principles and conceptual models. It is expected that many countries that have used AACR2 will probably implement RDA. Some countries that have used their own national cataloging codes have watched RDA's development with interest, with the possibility that they will consider adopting RDA.

NOTES

1. ONIX = ONline Information eXchange, an international standard of the publishing industry. See www.editeur.org/74/FAQs/.

2. IFLA Study Group on the Functional Requirements for Bibliographic Records, *Functional Requirements for Bibliographic Records* (Munich: Saur, 1998). Also online: www.ifla.org/en/ publications/functional-requirements-for-bibliographicrecords/.

3. Olivia Madison,"Utilizing the FRBR Framework in Designing User-Focused Digital Content and Access Systems," *Library Resources & Technical Services* 50, no. 1 (2006): 15.

4. Pat Riva, "Introducing the Functional Requirements for Bibliographic Records and Related IFLA Developments," *Bulletin of the American Society for Information Science & Technology* 33, no. 6 (2007): 9–10, www.asis.org/Bulletin/Aug-07/Riva.pdf.

5. FRBR Review Group, "FRBR Bibliography," www.ifla.org/en/node/881/.

6. IFLA Meetings of Experts on an International Cataloguing Code (IME-ICC), "Statement of International Cataloguing Principles, 2009," www.ifla.org/files/cataloguing/icp/icp _2009-en.pdf.

7. Ibid.

3

FRBR AND FRAD
IN RDA

RDA is an application of the FRBR and FRAD conceptual models. RDA itself is not a conceptual model, but rather a set of practical instructions based on the FRBR and FRAD models. These models have shaped the structure of RDA and influenced the language used in the instructions. Some background knowledge of these models helps to explain the nature of RDA and how it differs from AACR2.

Browsing through the table of contents of RDA, it is immediately apparent that the structure and language of RDA are different from AACR2:

> Section 1—Recording attributes of manifestation and item
>
> Section 2—Recording attributes of work and expression
>
> Section 3—Recording attributes of person, family, and corporate body
>
> Section 4—Recording attributes of concept, object, event, and place
>
> Section 5—Recording primary relationships
>
> Section 6—Recording relationships to persons, families, and corporate bodies associated with a resource
>
> Section 7—Recording the subject of a work
>
> Section 8—Recording relationships between works, expressions, manifestations, and items
>
> Section 9—Recording relationships between persons, families, and corporate bodies
>
> Section 10—Recording relationships between concepts, objects, events, and places

Where does this vocabulary come from? Where do the concepts and categories come from? They come from the FRBR and FRAD conceptual models. The following section gives a brief overview of the models and an introduction to the models' concepts and vocabulary.

OVERVIEW OF FRBR AND FRAD
Origins of FRBR and FRAD

The FRBR conceptual model has its origin in the report of a group appointed by IFLA, the International Federation of Library Associations and Institutions. In the early 1990s, the IFLA Cataloguing Section appointed a study group to examine the functional requirements of bibliographic records. This group had representation from many different countries. They carried out an extensive study over several years that also included a period for worldwide review. In 1997, the final report was approved by IFLA's Standing Committee on Cataloguing and published the subsequent year with the title *Functional Requirements for Bibliographic Records: Final Report.*[1]

The final report contains the description of the entity relationship model that the study group developed to analyze bibliographic records and make their recommendations (FRBR 2.1).

> The study has two primary objectives. The first is to provide a clearly defined, structured framework for relating the data that are recorded in bibliographic records to the needs of the users of those records. The second objective is to recommend a basic level of functionality for records created by national bibliographic agencies.

The development of a framework or model was one of two objectives, but it is the model that has continued to be discussed and applied. The international cataloging community quickly recognized the validity of the model. The model became the common, shared language for discussions of cataloging and cataloging revision, and the basis for new research and applications. IFLA decided to appoint new groups to extend the FRBR model to include authority data (Functional Requirements for Authority Data, FRAD), and subject authority data (Functional Requirements for Subject Authority Data, FRSAD). The Working Group on Functional Requirements and Numbering of Authority Records (FRANAR) developed the FRAD model, and their final report was published in 2009.[2] FRSAD is in the process of being developed, with a first draft issued in 2008, and a second draft in 2009.[3] IFLA also decided to establish the FRBR Review Group to review and maintain the FRBR family of conceptual models and to encourage their application.[4]

Focus on the User

The FRBR and FRAD models are entity relationship models. They were developed using a similar approach and methodology. Users and their needs are the starting point for both models. The first step is to identify "key objects that are of interest to users of information in a particular domain" (FRBR 2.3 and FRAD 3.1). The models map out the relationship between the data that is recorded—in either bibliographic or authority records—and the needs of those who use that data.

The needs of the user are defined in terms of user tasks. The FRBR user tasks are "generic tasks that are performed by users when searching and making use of national bibliographies and library catalogues" (FRBR 2.2). FRBR does not make a distinction between the end user and the library or information worker who assists the end user. The FRAD user tasks also address the needs of users, but in this case, two classes of users are identified: the end user and those who assist the end user by creating and maintaining authority data. The end user is listed as the second category (FRAD 6):

- authority data creators who create and maintain authority files;

- users who use authority information either through direct access to author-ity files or indirectly through the controlled access points (authorized forms, variant forms of names/references, etc.) in catalogues, national bibliogra-phies, other similar databases, etc.

The FRBR and FRAD models look at data within the context of large catalogs or databases. The user tasks are tasks associated with navigating through large amounts of data in order to discover and obtain the required resource. There are four user tasks associated with the use of bibliographic data, and four tasks for authority data. Since the tasks address the use of two different types of data, the tasks are not identical, but they do overlap.

The four user tasks associated with bibliographic data, as defined by the FRBR Study Group (FRBR 6.1), are

Find	to *find* entities that correspond to the user's stated search criteria (i.e., to locate either a single entity or a set of entities in a file or database as the result of a search using an attribute or relationship of the entity);
Identify	to *identify* an entity (i.e., to confirm that the entity described corresponds to the entity sought, or to distinguish between two or more entities with similar characteristics);
Select	to *select* an entity that is appropriate to the user's needs (i.e., to choose an entity that meets the user's requirements with respect to content, physical format, etc., or to reject an entity as being inappropriate to the user's needs);
Obtain	to acquire or *obtain* access to the entity described (i.e., to acquire an entity through purchase, loan, etc., or to access an entity electronically through an online connection to a remote computer).

These are recognizable tasks that users perform. For example, if a user needs to read Defoe's *Robinson Crusoe,* he starts a search in an online catalog with a search term, such as the name of the author or the title. He starts by trying to find something that matches his search term. If he has input the title, *Robinson Crusoe,* he looks at the results to identify what matches his query. If it's only one result, is it what he wanted? Other resources may have the same title, but he does not want adaptations, or parodies, or criticisms; he wants the original text by Defoe. If there are many results, then he identifies the ones that correspond to what he wants. Once he has identified one or several manifestations that contain the original text of *Robinson Crusoe*, he needs to select the one that fits his needs. Supposing that he is a student completing a term paper at a time when the library building is closed, he may only be interested in electronic books. Once he has selected what he wants, the last step is actually using the sought resource, either by obtaining it on a shelf or, in the case of electronic resources, connecting to it and accessing it online.

The four user tasks associated with authority data, as defined by the FRANAR Working Group (FRAD 6), are as follows:

Find	Find an entity or set of entities corresponding to stated criteria (i.e., to find either a single entity or a set of entities using an attribute or combination of attributes or a relationship of the entity as the search criteria); or to explore the universe of bibliographic entities using those attributes and relationships.
Identify	Identify an entity (i.e., to confirm that the entity represented corresponds to the entity sought, to distinguish between two or more entities with similar characteristics) or to validate the form of name to be used as a controlled access point.
Contextualize	Place a person, corporate body, work, etc. in context; clarify the relationship between two or more persons, corporate bodies, works, etc.; or clarify the relationship between a person, corporate body, etc. and a name by which that person, corporate body, etc. is known (e.g., name used in religion versus secular name).
Justify	Document the authority data creator's reason for choosing the name or form of name on which a controlled access point is based.

The user tasks "find" and "identify" are common to both models, and their definitions are similar, except in FRAD they are tasks involving authority data. Again, the tasks are frequently performed and recognizable. For example, the user starts by looking for an author, using the author's name. The user may simply want to retrieve everything associated with the author's name, or may use that as a starting point to navigate to other related resources, to other persons related to the author, etc. If there were three or four different authors with the name Daniel Defoe, the user would need to identify which one is the Daniel Defoe he needs. From a cataloger's perspective, to identify is to validate the form of the name. To contextualize and justify are not universal user tasks; they are tasks carried out by those who create authority data for the benefit of the end user. To contextualize is to clarify relationships, for example, the relationship between earlier and later names of a corporate body: the National Library of Canada and the National Archives of Canada merged in 2003 to form Library and Archives Canada. To justify is to record the reasons that justify choosing to use the name Daniel Defoe or Library and Archives Canada in controlled access points.

The FRBR and FRAD conceptual models are based on a detailed analysis of bibliographic and authority data. They set forth a framework for understanding the bibliographic universe. The models shift the cataloging world's perspective because they look at bibliographic data from the user's perspective. The focus is not on the cataloger creating a single record, but on the user seeking that record within the context of a large catalog or database. Both activities continue to coexist, but the defining perspective has changed. The data that is analyzed is data of interest to the user because it enables the user to accomplish one of the basic user tasks. The models promote a view of the bibliographic universe where the focus is on what is important to the user. Cataloging principles and cataloging codes have always aimed to serve the needs of the user, sometimes explicitly stating this goal, sometimes implying it. For example, Charles A. Cutter, in 1876, did explicitly state, in his *Rules for a Printed Dictionary Catalog,* that the objective of the catalog was to help the user: "to enable a person to find a book . . . to show what the library has . . . and to assist in the choice of a book"[5] S. R. Ranganathan, with his five laws of library science first published in 1931, also underlined the basic principle that we organize information for the benefit of the user: "books are for use; every person his or her book; every book its reader; save the time of the reader; a library is a growing organism."[6] The FRBR and FRAD models continue in this tradition of focusing on the user, but they go further by providing a detailed analysis of the way in which each attribute and relationship that is recorded in a bibliographic or authority record is relevant and important to the user.

FRBR Entities, Attributes, and Relationships

FRBR Entities

There are three components in an entity relationship model: entities, attributes or characteristics of the entities, and relationships between the entities.

The FRBR entities are the objects of interest to users of bibliographic data: the products of intellectual or artistic creation; the persons or corporate bodies responsible for playing some role with respect to those products; and the subjects of those products of intellectual and artistic creation.

The FRBR model identifies three groups of entities:

Group 1 entities: products of intellectual or artistic endeavour
                      entities: work, expression, manifestation, item

Group 2 entities:	those responsible for the intellectual or artistic content, the physical production and dissemination, or the custodianship of the entities in the first group **entities:** persons, corporate bodies
Group 3 entities:	subjects **entities:** concept, object, event, place + all the entities in groups 1 and 2

The group 2 and 3 entities are fairly self-explanatory. The group 1 entities present a challenge because they are both straightforward and puzzling. The terms *work, manifestation,* and *item* are familiar terms. The FRBR model uses these terms and precisely defines the scope and meaning of each term. The model also defines the entity *expression,* adding an important layer between work and manifestation.

The group 1 entities do not exist as separate, tangible objects. The four entities are aspects that correspond to a user's interests in the products of intellectual and artistic creation (FRBR 3.1.1). The definition of each entity is inextricably intertwined with the definition of the other group 1 entities:

work:	a distinct intellectual or artistic creation
expression:	the intellectual or artistic realization of a work in the form of alpha-numeric, musical, or choreographic notation, sound, image, object, movement, etc., or any combination of such forms
manifestation:	the physical embodiment of an expression of a work
item:	a single exemplar of a manifestation

The definitions of the group 1 entities demonstrate the primary relationships that exist between these four entities. Figure 3.1 (from section 3.1.1 of the FRBR report) illustrates these relationships. The diagram looks like a simple hierarchy, but the arrows are important because they indicate that there is a network of relationships. Some relationships are one to many, some are many to many. One work can be realized through one or more expressions. But an expression realizes only one work. An expression can be embodied in many different manifestations, and a manifestation can be the embodiment of one or more expressions. A manifestation is usually exemplified by many items, though it can also be exemplified by a single item. An item can only be the exemplar of one manifestation.

One can use a real example, such as Daniel Defoe's *Robinson Crusoe,* to illustrate the relationships between the group 1 entities, as shown in figure 3.2. The group 1 entities do not exist separately: the copy of *Robinson Crusoe* that I am reading is an item, a single physical copy that belongs to McGill University and carries the barcode number 31025693698. At the same time, it is also the exemplar of a particular manifestation,

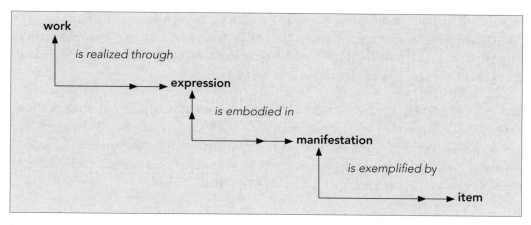

FIGURE 3.1

FRBR group 1 entities and primary relationships (from FRBR 3.1.1)

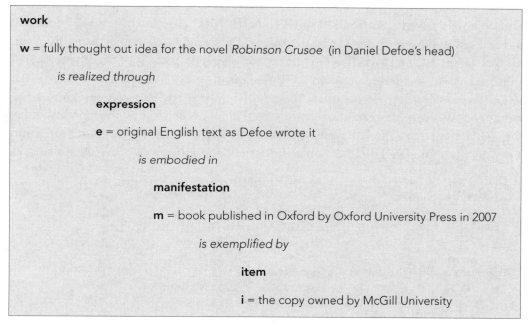

FIGURE 3.2

Group 1 entities and primary relationships with *Robinson Crusoe* as the example

i.e., the Oxford University Press manifestation published in 2007. That manifestation embodies a particular expression, the original English-language text, and that alphanumeric expression was the first realization of Defoe's work. The book in my hand has all four aspects: item, manifestation, expression, and work.

The group 2 entities are the entities that are responsible for the creation of a work, realization of an expression, production or dissemination of a manifestation, or ownership of an item. The FRBR model identifies two group 2 entities: persons and corporate bodies. The FRAD model, which will be discussed in more detail below, takes as its starting point the set of bibliographic entities defined in the FRBR model. The FRAD model makes one modification: it expands the group 2 entities to include family as well. Descriptions of the FRBR model now often assume the FRAD definition of group 2 entities: person, family, and corporate body.[7]

The group 3 entities are the subjects of the group 1 entities. This group includes four entities that are specific to this group: concept, object, event, and place. It also includes all the group 1 and group 2 entities because these too can be the subjects of works. An event, such as the Battle of Hastings, can be the subject of a work. A work, such as Defoe's *Robinson Crusoe,* can also be the subject of another work.

FRBR Attributes

Each entity has a set of characteristics or attributes. The entity is a key object of interest to the user. It is an abstract organizing category around which to cluster certain types of data. The attributes of an entity are the data that are used to find, identify, select, and obtain a resource. Attributes can be "inherent" or "externally imputed." Inherent attributes are attributes that can be discovered by directly examining the entity itself, such as extent, the title found on the title page of a printed book, type of content, date of publication, etc. Externally imputed attributes are attributes that come from outside the entity, such as an assigned identifier. Externally imputed attributes often require using a reference source—for example, consulting a thematic index to find the thematic index number assigned to a musical composition (FRBR 4.1). Examples of attributes for group 1 entities are shown in figure 3.3. Some attributes have widespread applicability, such as

Attributes of an item	item identifier (e.g., barcode number) provenance of the item marks/inscriptions etc.
Attributes of a manifestation	publisher/distributor date of publication/distribution form of carrier extent of the carrier etc.
Attributes of an expression	form of expression language of expression type of score (musical notation) scale (cartographic image/object) etc.
Attributes of a work	form of work medium of performance (musical work) coordinates (cartographic work) etc.

FIGURE 3.3

Examples of attributes for group 1 entities

title and *date*. Other attributes only apply to certain types of resources, such as *scale* and *projection* for cartographic resources.

Group 2 and 3 entities also have their particular attributes. In the FRBR model, the attributes of person are names, dates, title (i.e., title as a term of address). The group 3 entities each have the attribute *term,* such as "economics" for concept or "ships" for object.

FRBR Relationships

An essential part of the FRBR model is the identification and mapping of relationships between the entities. Relationships play a very important role in assisting the user to complete the tasks of finding, identifying, selecting, and obtaining and are the key to navigating through the bibliographic universe. They carry information about the nature of the links that exist between entities, enable collocation, and provide pathways to improve resource discovery. By focusing attention on bibliographic relationships and relating each relationship to the user tasks, the FRBR model emphasizes the role that bibliographic relationships play when a user navigates a large catalog or database.

The FRBR model looks at the relationships between the groups of entities. For example, there are the familiar relationships between group 1 and 2 entities:

Group 1 entity	Relationship	Group 2 entity
work	*created by*	person
expression	*translated by*	person
manifestation	*published by*	corporate body
item	*owned by*	family

Likewise, there are subject relationships. Subject relationships can relate any group 1, 2, or 3 entity to a work.

Entity	Relationship	Entity
event (group 3)	*subject of*	work
person (group 2)	*subject of*	work
work A (group 1)	*subject of*	work B

The FRBR model also focuses attention on the relationships between the group 1 entities. The primary (or logical relationships at a high level of generalization) are the relationships between one work and its expressions, manifestations, and items. The primary relationships between group 1 entities were already evident in the definition of the group 1 entities: an item is the exemplar of a manifestation, which is the embodiment of an expression, which is the realization of a work.[8]

A work is often realized in only one expression. But works that have formed an important part of our cultural and intellectual history are usually realized in many expressions. A work, such as *Robinson Crusoe,* has many expressions. Some expressions are translations of the original English text into other languages, such as French and German translations. Some expressions may be realizations into a different form of expression—for example, a spoken word version instead of one in alpha-numeric notation. Each expression may be published in several manifestations, and each manifestation usually has a number of identical exemplars of the manifestation.

Even if a work has only one expression, it is still important to identify both the work and expression entities. Expression is an important entity because it adds a degree of precision in the delineation of similarities and differences between the content of resources. Manifestations of the same expression embody identical content, though the manifestations are different: for example, identical content but different dates of publication, different extent, etc. Manifestations of different expressions are still related to each other because they are related to the same work, but they embody slightly different content because they embody different realizations of the work. For example, revised editions have slightly different content. They are realizations of the same work, but the expressions are not identical. Translations are realizations of the same content, but every word is different.

Work and expression are entities that pertain to content. By having four group 1 entities, the FRBR model provides a way to be more precise about the similarities and differences in content and the degree of relationship that exists between resources that embody the same work. For example, *Robinson Crusoe* can be expressed in alpha-numeric notation or in spoken word. These are two expressions of the same work because the content is the same, even though it is realized using different forms of expression. However, a screenplay or a film adaptation would be a related work, different from the original work, but with a relationship to the original. The screenplay would have a relationship of transformation. The film would have a relationship of adaptation.

This added degree of precision is important for the fulfillment of user tasks, especially the tasks of identifying and selecting the appropriate resource. The work and expression entities enable the collocation of content that is the same, and the identification of content that realizes the same work but may be a slightly different realization. A user can be led to identical content in different manifestations, and can also be shown the same content available in different realizations or expressions.

FRBR also maps out the relationships between group 1 entities of different works. There are several types of whole-part relationships because the whole-part relationship can happen at the work, expression, manifestation, or item level. There are also a large number of relationships between different works, relationships such as imitation, adaptation, transformation, supplement, successor, etc.

These bibliographic relationships are not new. However, the level of information recorded about bibliographic relationships and about the exact nature of those relationships has varied over time and in different cataloging contexts. The FRBR model focuses attention on the importance of recording the existence of a relationship, and also on the importance of identifying the exact nature of the relationship. Clarifying bibliographic relationships is key to the completion of user tasks, especially in the current context of large catalogs and databases.

FRAD Entities, Attributes, and Relationships

FRAD Entities

The FRAD model extends the FRBR model. FRAD includes all the FRBR entities and has additional entities specific to authority control. The entities defined in the FRBR model—the group 1, 2, and 3 entities—are collectively called the "bibliographic entities." The entities specific to FRAD are name, identifier, controlled access point, rules, and agency. The user of a catalog may be less directly aware of the entities associated with authority control, yet these entities are important because they support collocation and navigation.

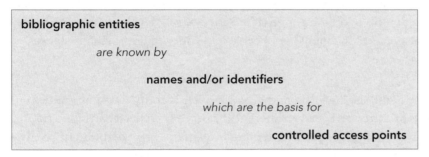

FIGURE 3.4

A simplified version of the FRAD model

FRAD also expands on the FRBR model by adding *family* to the group 2 entities and introducing more granularity. A simplified version (based on figure 1 in FRAD section 3.3) is shown in figure 3.4. Bibliographic entities are known by names or are assigned identifiers. Names and identifiers are the basis for controlled access points. The formulation of controlled access points is governed by rules that are applied by agencies. [9] Agencies create or modify controlled access points.

The FRAD model makes one important change from the FRBR model. The name of a person and the title of a work are no longer considered attributes. Instead, the entity *name* is identified. FRAD 3.4 defines *name* as follows:

A character or group of words and/or characters by which an entity is known in the real world.

> Includes names by which persons, families, and corporate bodies are known.
>
> Includes titles by which works, expressions, manifestations, and items are known.
>
> Includes names and terms by which concepts, objects, events, and places are known.
>
> Includes real names, pseudonyms, religious names, initials, and separate letters, numerals, or symbols.
>
> [The list continues for more than two pages.]

If name is a separate entity, then the name and the person have a relationship, or the name and the work have a relationship. At first glance, it may appear a needless complication. Actually, it simplifies the conceptual model because it accommodates more complex relationships and different concepts of bibliographic identity. A person is "an individual or a persona established or adopted by an individual or group" (FRAD 3.4). One individual may have many personas; several people may together adopt a single persona. Different cataloging traditions treat personas and the pseudonyms used by personas in different ways.[10] With name as a separate entity, the FRAD model builds in more flexibility to identify and define a broader range of relationships between names and entities, and also makes the model applicable in a wider range of circumstances.

FRAD Attributes

For the bibliographic entities, the FRBR and FRAD models identify the same entities but define different sets of attributes because different attributes are reflected in bibliographic data versus authority data. Though the two models overlap, they are different because they each focus on different portions of the bibliographic universe.

In the FRBR model, the attributes that are defined include only those that usually are part of bibliographic data. For example, for the entity *person*, the FRBR attributes are as follows (FRBR 4.6):

name of *person*	dates of *person*
title of *person*	other designation associated with the *person*

The FRAD model, reflecting data required for authority control, has a long list of possible attributes for the entity *person*, attributes that can be found in authority data. Thus, in FRAD, the attributes listed for person are as follows (FRAD 4.1):

dates associated with the person	place of death*
title of person	country*
gender*	place of residence*
place of birth*	affiliation*

address*	biography/history*
language of person*	other information associated with
field of activity*	the person
profession/occupation*	

The attributes with asterisks are those that are not in the FRBR model. These additional attributes are important for identifying the person, clarifying who the person is, and distinguishing the person from other persons.

The lists of attributes for group 1 entities are also different in the two models. There are more attributes listed in FRBR than in FRAD. Notes in FRAD confirm and explain the divergence. For example, here is the note that appears at the end of the FRAD list of attributes of a work (FRAD 4.4):

> Note: The attributes of a work listed above include only those that are normally reflected in controlled access points or in other data elements recorded in authority records. They do not include other attributes of a work that may be reflected in bibliographic records, as identified in Functional Requirements for Bibliographic Records.

FRAD Relationships

The FRAD model also puts a strong emphasis on the role of relationships between entities. One of the basic relationships is that between a name or identifier and one of the bibliographic entities:

Bibliographic entity	Relationship	FRAD entity
person	*has appellation*	name
work	*has appellation*	name
corporate body	*is assigned*	identifier
manifestation	*is assigned*	identifier

In the FRAD model, the relationships are organized into four categories. The first category covers relationships between the group 1 and 2 bibliographic entities, as well as the general relationships between the FRAD entities: bibliographic entities, names, identifiers, controlled access points, rules, and agencies.

The other three categories are the relationships expressed in the authority reference structure. This is a simplified summary of the categories:

1. relationships between entities: relationships between persons, families, corporate bodies, and relationships among works

    - the *see also* reference structure[11]

2. relationships between the names of an entity

- the *see* reference structure

3. relationships between controlled access points

- two or more access points for the same entity; for example, parallel language, alternate scripts, different rules, etc.

The relationships that FRAD identifies are familiar relationships, relationships that are easily recognized as the basis for authority control work. For example, some of the relationships between a person and other entities include

Entity	Relationship	Entity
person	pseudonymous	person (persona)
person	membership	corporate body
person	official	person (identity in an official capacity, e.g., president or prime minister)

As was the case with attributes, there is also an overlap between FRBR and FRAD relationships. For example, FRBR and FRAD both map out the relationships between different works—relationships such as imitation, adaptation, transformation, supplement, and successor. FRBR's aim is to identify the nature of bibliographic relationships. FRAD looks at how these relationships are expressed in authority data. Thus, for the adaptation relationship, FRBR identifies it as a type of relationship that can exist between two works, between a work and an expression, and between expressions. FRAD identifies how the relationship is expressed in the *see also* reference structure, in information notes that may be part of an authority record, and in the controlled access point in the bibliographic record.

Why Are FRBR and FRAD Important?

FRBR and FRAD give us a way to understand and talk about the bibliographic universe. They are based on the analysis of actual bibliographic and authority data. The models give a cohesive and logically sound representation of the nature of bibliographic and authority data. The entities, attributes, and relationships are a useful way of organizing our understanding of the bibliographic universe.

It is still the same bibliographic universe that existed before FRBR and FRAD. Taking a MARC record from the 1980s, well before the development of the FRBR model, we can easily examine it through a FRBR perspective and identify FRBR entities, attributes, and relationships, as shown in figure 3.5. Bibliographic data has not changed. The FRBR family of conceptual models introduces a systematic and coherent framework for understanding the nature of this data. The framework also provides a common vocabulary and conceptual language that is recognized internationally.

020	$a 0521361834	manifestation identifier
100 1	$a Montesquieu, Charles-Louis de Secondat, $c baron de La Brède et de, $d 1689-1755	person "created by" relationship to the work
240	10 $a De l'esprit des lois. $l English	$a =work $ l = expression
245	14 $a The spirit of the laws / $c Montesquieu ; translated and edited by Anne M. Cohler, Basia Carolyn Miller, Harold Samuel Stone.	manifestation
260	$a Cambridge ; $a New York : $b Cambridge University Press, $c 1989	manifestation
300	$a xlvii, 757 p. : $b ill. ; $c 22 cm.	manifestation
500	$a Translation of: De l'esprit des lois.	expression
650 0	$a Political science	concept "subject of" relationship to the work
650 0	$a State, The	
650 0	$a Law $x Philosophy	
700 1	$a Cohler, Anne M.	person "realized by" relationship to this expression
700 1	$a Miller, Basia Carolyn.	
700 1	$a Stone, Harold Samuel, ǀd 1949	

FIGURE 3.5

Identifying FRBR entities and relationships in a MARC record

FRBR and FRAD identify the key components of bibliographic and authority data and assess the value of each component in accomplishing user tasks. The models promote a change in perspective because the data is analyzed in terms of its utility for those who will use the data. The models also take the perspective of navigating through large catalogs and databases. The focus is not a single record but the sum of bibliographic and authority data in large catalogs and databases.

Since the models clarify the underlying structure of bibliographic and authority data, they can play a significant role in the process of developing and revising cataloging standards. They act as a basic road map. They can be used as the reference point against which to measure and test that cataloging instructions are comprehensive and consistent and to evaluate if the instructions produce effective metadata that corresponds to user needs.

The FRBR model also presents a clear way to conceptually separate content and carrier. FRBR's separation into four group 1 entities— work, expression, manifestation, and item— allows for a more precise definition of the boundaries between content and carrier. Work and expression are about content; manifestation and item are about carriers. Content is not assumed to be a single entity, work, but is differentiated into two entities, work and expression. This differentiation allows for a clearer definition of the relationship between content that is similar but not identical. In some cases, the same work in a different expression may satisfy the user's need, but in other cases, a user may need a particular expression. For example, a user with a visual impairment may only be able to access the content of *Robinson Crusoe* through a spoken word expression. The identification of two content entities, work and expression, allows for a more precise collocation and display of search results. This conceptual separation is important because the degree of similarity in content is important to users and enables users to find, identify, and select the resource that is most appropriate to their needs.

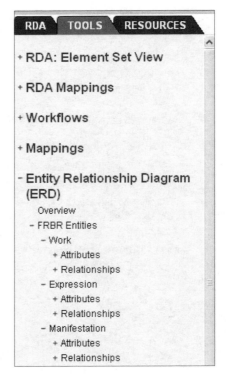

FIGURE 3.6

Entity relationship diagrams are included in the RDA Toolkit (June 2010)

EVIDENCE OF FRBR AND FRAD IN RDA

When we look at RDA with an awareness of the FRBR and FRAD models, it is easy to see evidence of RDA's alignment with the models and to understand the rationale for RDA's content and the organization of that content. This section will look at a few fundamental aspects that demonstrate the alignment.

Entity Relationship Diagrams

The easiest way to visualize the connection between RDA and the FRBR and FRAD models is to look at the entity relationship diagrams (ERDs) that form part of the RDA Toolkit (figure 3.6). The diagrams are like a road map for RDA. The diagrams start from the FRBR and FRAD entities, and display the attributes and relationships associated with each entity.

The diagrams give visual confirmation of RDA's alignment with the conceptual models. The diagrams are firstly diagrams of RDA content. Looking at the diagram of the core attributes of the work entity (figure 3.7), we can see that the diagram gives an outline of RDA, mapping all the elements that are core attributes at the work level.[12]

The diagram does not intend to match the sequence and numbering of the instructions as seen when we browse the table of contents. But it does cover all the relevant attributes—in this case, all the core attributes of work. The terms in the diagram are the terms used in RDA, and the attributes are all the attributes covered by RDA instructions. For each attribute, the diagram also includes a reference to the documents describing the FRBR and FRAD models, demonstrating and confirming the alignment between RDA and the models. There are cases where RDA includes additional attributes, such as Signatory to a Treaty, Etc., which were not explicitly listed as attributes in the original FRBR and FRAD models. In other diagrams, one can see that RDA breaks down an attribute into more detail than in the conceptual models, as in Numbering of Serials (figure 3.8). Numbering of serials is an FRBR attribute. RDA has an element for numbering of serials. RDA's element is further broken down into sub-elements. This diagram shows four of the eight possible subelements.

RDA is a set of practical instructions based on FRBR and FRAD. In places, RDA includes more details than the models. The entity relationship diagrams give a visual overview of RDA and also confirm the alignment between RDA and the FRBR and FRAD models.

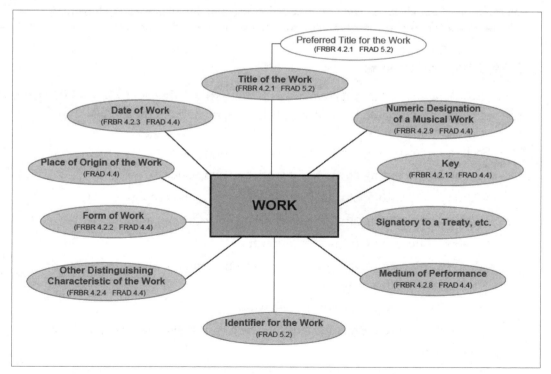

FIGURE 3.7

ERD: Core attributes of work (minus the details for medium of performance), as shown in the RDA Toolkit (June 2010)

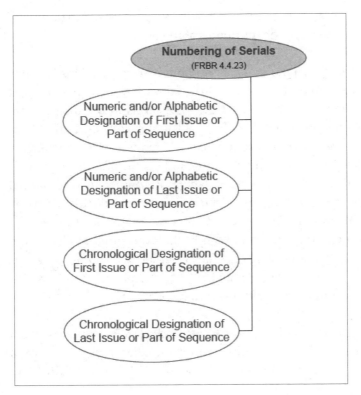

FIGURE 3.8

Numbering of Serials (as shown in the RDA Toolkit, June 2010) illustrating how RDA elements are sometimes more detailed than the original FRBR attribute.

RDA Table of Contents

When browsing RDA's table of contents with some knowledge of FRBR and FRAD, one can recognize the vocabulary and concepts that originate from the models:

Section 1—Recording attributes of manifestation and item

Section 2—Recording attributes of work and expression

Section 3—Recording attributes of person, family, and corporate body

Section 4—Recording attributes of concept, object, event, and place

Section 5—Recording primary relationships

Section 6—Recording relationships to persons, families, and corporate bodies associated with a resource

Section 7—Recording the subject of a work

Section 8—Recording relationships between works, expressions, manifestations, and items

Section 9—Recording relationships between persons, families, and corporate bodies

Section 10—Recording relationships between concepts, objects, events, and places

RDA instructions are organized into sections, and the sections are separated according to the FRBR bibliographic entities. The first four sections of RDA focus on recording the attributes of bibliographic entities, and sections 5 through 10 focus on recording relationships between entities.

The sections that map to the group 3 entities, subjects, are mostly placeholders,[13] and are included in the structure of RDA in order to have a complete mapping between the FRBR family of models[14] and RDA. The placeholders are areas that may be developed in the future.

User Tasks

If we look at the structure within the sections of RDA, we find more evidence of its alignment with FRBR and FRAD. The chapter structure within each section is aligned with the FRBR and FRAD user tasks. Each section begins with a chapter of general guidelines. The remaining chapters are organized according to the user tasks. Each chapter includes instructions that support one of the user tasks.

For example, the chapters in section 1 are organized according to the FRBR tasks identify, select, and obtain:

Section 1—Recording attributes of manifestation and item
Chapter 1—General guidelines
Chapter 2—Identifying manifestations and items *FRBR task = Identify*
Chapter 3—Describing carriers *FRBR task = Select*
Chapter 4—Providing acquisition and access information *FRBR task = Obtain*

The chapters in section 9 include instructions for recording data to support authority control. The chapters are separated according to the group 2 entities. Since the section focuses on data to support authority control, all the chapters are associated with the same user task, find.

Section 9—Recording relationships between persons, families, and corporate bodies
Chapter 29—General guidelines
Chapter 30—Related persons *FRAD task = Find*
Chapter 31—Related families *FRAD task = Find*
Chapter 32—Related corporate bodies *FRAD task = Find*

The chapter of general guidelines is the starting point in every section. The general guidelines always include a part called "Functional Objectives and Principles." The functional objectives relate the instructions of the section back to the user tasks, reinforcing the link between the data that is recorded and the role of the data in completing a user task.

For example, functional objectives and principles for section 1 are

> **1.2** *Functional Objectives and Principles*
>
> The data describing a manifestation or item should enable the user to:
>
> a) *find* manifestations and items that correspond to the user's stated search criteria
>
> b) *identify* the resource described (i.e., confirm that the resource described corresponds to the resource sought, or distinguish between two or more resources with the same or similar characteristics)
>
> c) *select* a resource that is appropriate to the user's requirements with respect to the physical characteristics of the carrier and the formatting and encoding of information stored on the carrier
>
> d) *obtain* a resource (i.e., acquire a resource through purchase, loan, etc., or access a resource electronically through an online connection to a remote computer).

The functional objectives and principles for section 9 are

> **29.2** *Functional Objectives and Principles*
>
> The data recorded to reflect relationships between persons, families, and corporate bodies should enable the user to:
>
> a) find persons, families, or corporate bodies that are related to the person, family, or corporate body represented by the data retrieved in response to the user's search
>
> b) understand the relationship between two or more persons, families, or corporate bodies.
>
> To ensure that the data created using RDA meet those functional objectives, the data should reflect all significant bibliographic relationships between persons, families, and corporate bodies represented by preferred access points and/or identifiers.

RDA uses the word *understand;* FRAD uses the word *contextualize;* the two represent the same user task.

Content of RDA Instructions

RDA adds many elements that were absent in AACR2. These are attributes and relationships that were identified in the FRBR and FRAD models and were judged to have a significant role in the successful completion of user tasks. Thus, the RDA chapter "Identifying Persons" gives instructions for recording data about all the attributes identified in the FRAD model:

9.	**Identifying Persons**
9.0	Purpose and Scope
9.1	General Guidelines on Identifying Persons
9.2	Name of the Person
9.3	Date Associated with the Person
9.4	Title of the Person
9.5	Fuller Form of Name
9.6	Other Designation Associated with the Person
9.7	Gender
9.8	Place of Birth
9.9	Place of Death
9.10	Country Associated with the Person
9.11	Place of Residence
9.12	Address of the Person
9.13	Affiliation
9.14	Language of the Person
9.15	Field of Activity of the Person
9.16	Profession or Occupation
9.17	Biographical Information
9.18	Identifier for the Person
9.19	Constructing Access Points to Represent Persons

The vocabulary that is used in RDA instructions reflects the concepts and terminology of the FRBR and FRAD models. For example, instead of instructions about "physical description," RDA instructions address the description of carriers. When we record an ISBN or ISSN, we are recording an identifier for the manifestation. Instead of "uniform titles," RDA distinguishes between an authorized access point representing a work and an authorized access point representing an expression. The term *heading* is absent from RDA. RDA uses the term *access point*.

Several instructions in RDA are basically the same as the AACR2 instruction. The intent and the end result are similar, but the wording has changed to reflect the vocabulary and concepts of the FRBR and FRAD models. In the following instruction, there is both a change in vocabulary and a change to align with the FRBR and FRAD models.

AACR2

25.8A

Use the collective title *Works* for an item that consists of, or purports to be, the complete works of a person, including those that are complete at the time of publication.

RDA

6.2.2.10.1

Record the conventional collective title *Works* as the preferred title for a compilation of works that consists of, or purports to be, the complete works of a person, family, or corporate body, including those that are complete at the time of publication.

The instruction has expanded from "complete works of a person" to complete works of all three of the group 2 entities: person, family, corporate body. The FRBR and FRAD conceptual models point out all the logical possibilities. Any group 2 entity may be responsible for intellectual or artistic content. Thus, this instruction should apply to the complete works of any group 2 entity. This instruction may rarely be applied in the case of a family or corporate body, but, to maintain logical consistency, it has been adjusted to encompass all three of the group 2 entities.

The FRBR and FRAD models underline the importance of relationships between bibliographic entities. The models not only identify the existence of many relationships, but also identify the types of relationships and demonstrate the importance of these relationships for the completion of user tasks. RDA puts a strong emphasis on the recording of relationships, with six sections of instructions for relationships. RDA significantly expands the use of relationship designators so that the precise type of relationships can be explicitly recorded. AACR2 had a short, optional rule at 21.0D. Instead, RDA includes full instructions on the use of relationship designators and three detailed appendices of terms:

Appendix I	Relationship Designators: Relationships Between a Resource and Persons, Families, and Corporate Bodies Associated with the Resource
Appendix J	Relationship Designators: Relationships Between Works, Expressions, Manifestations, and Items
Appendix K	Relationship Designators: Relationships Between Persons, Families, and Corporate Bodies[15]

The concepts and vocabulary of the FRBR and FRAD models played an important role in shaping RDA. One can use RDA without background knowledge of the models, but some knowledge of the concepts and vocabulary makes it easier to see the rationale for RDA's content and its shape and structure.

NOTES

1. IFLA Study Group on the Functional Requirements for Bibliographic Records, *Functional Requirements for Bibliographic Records* (Munich: Saur, 1998). Also online: www.ifla.org/en/publications/functional-requirements-for-bibliographic-records/.

2. IFLA Working Group on Functional Requirements and Numbering of Authority Records (FRANAR), *Functional Requirements for Authority Data : A Conceptual Model* (Munich: Saur, 2009).

3. IFLA Working Group on Functional Requirements of Subject Authority Records (FRASAR), "Functional Requirements for Subject Authority Data," 2nd draft (June 10, 2009), www.ifla.org/en/node/1297/.

4. FRBR Review Group, "About the FRBR Review Group," www.ifla.org/en/about-the-frbr-review-group/.

5. Charles A. Cutter. *Rules for a Printed Dictionary Catalog,* 4th ed. (Washington, DC: Government Printing Office, 1904),12. Also online (digitized by University of North Texas Digital Collections): http://digital.library.unt.edu/permalink/meta-dc-1048/.

6. S. R. Ranganathan, *The Five Laws of Library Science* (Madras, India: Madras Library Association, 1931).

7. Barbara Tillett, "The Influence of FRBR on RDA" (presented at the 2008 ALA Annual Conference session "Getting Ready for RDA"), http://presentations.ala.org/images/1/1e/Getting_ready_for_RDA_FRBR_influences_2008rev_color.pdf.

8. The relationships between the group 1 entities are sometimes called "inherent" because the nature of the relationship is essentially the definition of the entity.

9. Entity definitions from FRAD 3.4:

   Controlled access point = A name, term, code, etc., under which a bibliographic or authority record or reference will be found. Includes access points designated as authorized (or preferred) forms of names . . . as well as variant forms of names . . .

   Rules = A set of instructions relating to the formulation and/or recording of controlled access points . . .

   Agency = An organization responsible for creating or modifying a controlled access point . . . Includes libraries, national bibliographic agencies, bibliographic utilities, consortia, museums, archives, rights management organizations, etc.

10. The note in FRAD gives a brief outline of two different approaches to pseudonyms. FRANAR, *Functional Requirements for Authority Data*, p. 25.

11. These relationships may also be expressed in the preferred form of a name or explanatory notes.

12. RDA defines certain attributes and relationships as "core elements." Elements are designated as core because they are essential to support the most basic user tasks. See RDA 0.6.1; also chapter 6 of this volume.

13. Sections 4, 7, and 10 are placeholders. Section 4 includes a small amount of content to cover the identification of place: chapter 16, "Identifying Places."

14. The FRBR family of models refers to the FRBR model and the extensions of the model to cover authority data, FRAD, and subject authority data, FRSAD.

15. There is a fourth placeholder appendix: "Relationship Designators: Relationships between Concepts, Objects, Events, and Places."

4

CONTINUITY WITH AACR2

RDA is the standard that replaces AACR2. RDA introduces significant changes, but important links continue to exist between AACR2 and RDA:

- AACR and RDA share the same governance structure.
- RDA was intentionally built on the foundations of AACR.
- Many RDA instructions are derived from AACR2.
- Cataloging records created according to RDA guidelines will be compatible with AACR records.
- RDA was born out of an initial attempt to do a radical revision of AACR.

SAME GOVERNANCE STRUCTURE

AACR was a cooperative venture that began with three author countries—Canada, Great Britain, and the United States—and then expanded to four when Australia joined at the beginning of the 1980s. There is a formal governance structure to manage both content development and publication, consisting of the Committee of Principals (CoP) that oversees all aspects; the Joint Steering Committee (JSC), which is responsible for the content of the standard and for the ongoing review and amendment of the standard; the Co-Publishers, who publish the work created by the Joint Steering Committee; and the Trustees or Fund Committee, which manage the financial aspects. Each of the committees has representation from the national libraries and the primary national library associations of each country.

During the transition to RDA, the governance structure and committees basically remain the same. The only change is the shift from the revision of AACR to the development of the new standard, RDA, which is notably reflected in the name change for the JSC: from the Joint Steering Committee for Revision of AACR to the Joint Steering Committee for Development of RDA.[1] After implementation, governance will be reviewed to consider the possibility of broader, international representation.

The Joint Steering Committee, the body responsible for the development of the content of AACR and then RDA, has representation from six organizations: the American Library Association, the Australian Committee on Cataloguing, the British Library, the Canadian Committee on Cataloguing, the Chartered Institute of Library and Information Professionals, and the Library of Congress. Each organization represents the cataloging constituencies in their respective countries. Thus, even if the JSC appears small, many voices are heard through the representatives. The JSC's method of operation can be characterized as consensus-building. All ideas are brought to the table and discussed, and decisions are reached through well-documented arguments.

One of AACR's strengths was the active and robust amending process which was administered by the Joint Steering Committee. AACR was originally developed in a print-based, card catalog environment. It was able to remain the cataloging standard that was in active use for decades because of the revision process. When there were changes in publication practices or when catalogers confronted new situations, AACR's amendment process kept the cataloging code up-to-date. With the advent of online catalogs and electronic resources, AACR2 went through many significant changes in order to respond to the challenges of the changing environment. At a certain point, it became evident that a total rewrite was required. Until that point, many problems had at least partially been addressed through the amendment process. The Joint Steering Committee will maintain the same ongoing development and amendment process with RDA. Already there is a list of issues that the JSC has deferred until after first release;[2] these will be addressed through the usual amendment process.

INTENTIONALLY BUILT ON THE FOUNDATIONS OF AACR

An initial question might be: why not begin with a totally blank slate and create something that is entirely new? The answer lies in the evidence that AACR was successful in fulfilling an important role and that it became a widely adopted standard. Thus, in developing a new standard, it made sense to build on the strengths of AACR.

During the twentieth century, library communities around the world made significant steps toward creating a coordinated international cataloging community. The *Paris Principles* of 1961 remains a landmark document in the history of cataloging because it represents the transformation from well-intentioned expressions of the desire to cooperate into a tangible road map for future harmonization. The *Paris Principles* provided a shaping structure for many cataloging codes around the world, including the *Anglo-American Cataloguing Rules* (AACR). The American, British, and Canadian cataloging communities, and subsequently also the Australian cataloging community, developed the set of cataloging rules known as AACR. AACR was their shared standard, but it also went on to be adopted more broadly. One can almost hear the element of surprise in the preface to the second edition:

> The starting point for this new edition is, indeed, the very clear success of the 1967 texts . . . not only in the three "Anglo-American" countries for which AACR was established, but throughout the world. AACR has been adopted . . . in most English-speaking countries, and has had a considerable influence on the formation or revision of local and national cataloguing rules in a number of others.[3]

AACR2 was translated into twenty-five different languages, demonstrating widespread adoption beyond the four author countries and beyond the other English-speaking countries.

With its widespread use around the world, AACR2 encouraged consistency in the recording of bibliographic data. This consistency enabled greater cooperation between cataloging agencies and institutions through an efficient sharing of records.

By following AACR, bibliographic data was formulated in ways that made sense to the user. AACR followed common usage and common citation practices, so the user had a sense of continuity rather than disconnect between different sources of bibliographic data, of which the catalog record might be one.

The Joint Steering Committee judged that it was not possible to achieve the required changes within the shell of AACR2, but it also recognized that there was much of value in the old standard. Thus the aim was to build "on foundations established by the *Anglo-American Cataloguing Rules* (AACR) and the cataloging traditions on which it was based." This aim appears both in the Strategic Plan[4] and in the opening chapter of the new standard (RDA, 0.2).

MANY RDA INSTRUCTIONS ARE DERIVED FROM AACR2

There are new instructions in RDA that have no equivalent in AACR2, and there are instructions that are changed and different in intent compared to their equivalent rule in AACR2. However, there are also many instructions where the wording is totally different but the intent of the instruction remains fundamentally the same. These instructions are "derived" from AACR2 and are "reworked."[5] The RDA instruction is given within the context of the FRBR/FRAD conceptual framework, using new vocabulary and concepts, in a new place within the structure of RDA. But, when I follow the instruction, the end result is that I record the same bibliographic data.

In some cases, the instruction is slightly reworded but remains identical:

AACR2

12.3B.   *Numeric and/or Alphabetic Designation*

12.3B1.

. . .

If the sequence of numbering is continued from a previous serial, give the numbering of the first issue or part of the serial represented by the new description.

RDA

2.6.2.3   *Recording Numeric and/or Alphabetic Designation of First Issue or Part of Sequence*

. . .

If the sequence of numeric and/or alphabetic designation is continued from a previous serial, record the numeric and/or alphabetic designation of the first issue or part of the serial represented by the new description.

In some cases, the intention and the net result of the instruction remain the same, but there is a difference in wording that reflects the new context for the instructions:

AACR2

1.1F4.

Transcribe a single statement of responsibility as such whether the two or more persons or corporate bodies named in it perform the same function or different functions.

RDA

2.4.1.5   *Statement Naming More Than One Person, Etc.*

Record a statement of responsibility naming more than one person, etc., as a single statement regardless of whether the persons, families, or corporate bodies named in it perform the same function or different functions.

In this case, the difference in wording is significant, not because it changes the intent of the instruction, but because the change demonstrates the alignment with the FRBR and FRAD conceptual models. The FRAD conceptual model identifies three entities that can have a relationship of responsibility for a resource: persons, families, and corporate bodies. The RDA instruction is expanded to include all three entities. The verb "record" is used, but one is, in effect, still transcribing the statement of responsibility, because the instructions on transcription appear in the preceding instruction, 2.4.1.4, Recording Statements of Responsibility. The placement of the instruction has also changed. It is in chapter 2, Identifying Manifestations and Items.

Many instructions are derived from AACR2 and maintain the intent of the original rule.

COMPATIBILITY OF RDA AND AACR2 RECORDS

In the "Strategic Plan for RDA, 2005–2009," there is recognition both of the need for change, and the need to maintain a certain level of continuity. The plan demonstrates the aim of building on the foundation of AACR. The plan also acknowledges the reality that when RDA is implemented, RDA records will need to coexist in databases full of AACR legacy records. Conscious awareness of the importance of compatibility between AACR and RDA data was translated into one of the long term goals:

> Be compatible with those descriptions and access points devised using AACR2, and present in existing catalogues and databases.[6]

There will be differences between AACR and RDA records. RDA includes many new elements that do not exist in AACR. The data recorded according to RDA is intended to support improved resource discovery, and thus it will be less ambiguous and more precisely segmented. For example, RDA encourages the careful identification of relationships and the recording of relationship designators so that the nature of a relationship can be readily ascertained by the user and so that the data about the relationship can be used by software to present a meaningful display of results.

In terms of description, there will be no necessity to change AACR records. However, as software evolves, it may be useful to add some of the new descriptive elements to older records to support more precise collocation with new RDA records and to improve the resource discovery experience for the user. It may be possible to develop and share machine algorithms or divide the work in collaborative projects to facilitate the upgrading of records.

The issue of compatibility is particularly critical when considering access points. The Joint Steering Committee did make some changes, but these cases were carefully scrutinized to ensure that any required modifications could be carried out with global updating procedures. For example, access points for individual books of the Bible were simplified. This was partly to simplify the formulation of the access points, and partly to move away from access points that reflect a Christian perspective of the Bible. The division of the Bible into the Old and New Testaments is a Christian way of aggregating the content. It does not make sense from a Jewish perspective. Thus, when referring to the Book of Genesis, the access point will eliminate the mention of the Old Testament:

> Bible. Genesis   *instead of*   Bible. O.T. Genesis

This change is also extended to individual New Testament books:

> Bible. Acts   *instead of*   Bible. N.T. Acts

This change will have an impact on indexes and display of data, but it is relatively simple to achieve with the global change functionality that most library databases have.

Other more complex changes, which would require human intervention on a case by case basis, were deferred in the interest of maintaining compatibility.

RDA WAS BORN OUT OF AN INITIAL ATTEMPT TO DO A RADICAL REVISION OF AACR

The history of RDA goes back to the need to address deep-seated problems in AACR. Even if there are many links between AACR and RDA, RDA is more than a revision of AACR. Not only have instructions and wording changed, but the instructions are applied within the context of a new theoretical framework. RDA's alignment with the two conceptual models, FRBR and FRAD, shapes the content of RDA and transforms it beyond a revision of AACR2.

One way to think about the development of RDA is to see it as the product of a process of deconstruction and then reconstruction around a new framework. Using the analogy of a major renovation project shows how the content of RDA and AACR2 are related and yet fundamentally different. This section will not be a comprehensive overview of the history of RDA's development, but will just look at the thread of deconstruction.

Up to the 1990s, the amendment process had proved to be sufficient in dealing with change. By the mid-1990s, with the proliferation of new publication practices, new electronic resources and new methods of scholarly and creative communication, it became increasingly clear that there were substantive issues beyond the scope of a simple amendment process. The Joint Steering Committee hosted a conference of experts to discuss the future direction of AACR. The International Conference on the Principles and Future Development of AACR, was held in Toronto, October 23–25, 1997. As a result of the conference, the Joint Steering Committee compiled a list of action items[7] and embarked on a process of revision that began within the AACR2 structure and then pushed beyond.

Two action items, in particular, began a process of revision that resulted in a complete deconstruction of AACR2:

> *Action:* Pursue the recommendation that a data modeling technique be used to provide a logical analysis of the principles and structures that underlie AACR.
>
> *Action:* Solicit a proposal to revise rule 0.24 to advance the discussion on the primacy of intellectual content over physical format.

The two action items overlap to a certain extent because they are both related to the "class of materials" concept. In AACR2, how a resource is described is determined by the class of material to which it belongs. The underlying assumption is that the categories in the class of materials concept are determined according to physical carrier. Both action items led to the conclusion that this assumption was incorrect and that the class of material concept was a major stumbling block to the flexibility and extensibility of AACR2.

The logical analysis was carried out by Tom Delsey and reported in the document "The Logical Structure of the Anglo-American Cataloguing Rules."[8] One of the fundamental problems in the logical structure of AACR was the categorization used in the class of materials concepts and for the general material designations. The assumption was that the categories were defined by physical carrier. However, on closer examination, it became clear that the categories were a mixture of content and carrier. For example, taking classes of material, only five classes are actually defined by physical carrier: sound recordings, motion pictures, videorecordings, computer files, and microforms. Cartographic material, graphic materials, and three-dimensional artifacts and realia are types of content, and these types of content are delivered on a variety of physical carriers, few of which are exclusive to one content type. For example, a photograph or a sheet can carry cartographic content or image content. Music, in the AACR context, is only music expressed through musical notation (i.e., scores) and does not include music that is recorded. Taking the FRBR model as a way to clarify the problem, we can see that some of the categories in the class of materials concept are defined according to attributes at the manifestation level, such as the class of material "videorecordings," defined according to media type; one class is defined according to an attribute at the expression level, form of expression i.e., music is really notated music (scores); some classes are defined according to an attribute at the work level, content type, e.g., cartographic material. With this mixture of categorizations, there is little wonder that it was difficult to extend AACR2 to describe new types of resources and difficult to describe resources consisting of different types of content. The recommendation in answer to this key issue was to consider the possibility of "deconstructing" class of materials and developing a more flexible approach, so that AACR could easily extend to the description of new types of resources. Since Part I of AACR2 was organized according to the class of materials, the way forward must also include deconstructing Part I. The recommendation was worded as "Use the model developed for this study to assess the options for restructuring Part I of the code."[9] Delsey also went on to suggest the possibility of reorganizing Part I according to the ISBD areas.

As early as 1999, work had begun on an experimental "alpha" prototype of a reorganized Part I of AACR2, created by Bruce Johnson and Bob Ewald. The prototype simply rearranged the rules, but it was the first step in the deconstruction process. It took the rules out of the structure based on class of materials chapters and organized them according to the ISBD areas. The rearrangement highlighted some problems and discrepancies. The ALA Task Force on Consistency across Part I of AACR2, was asked to analyze the consistency of rules across the chapters in Part I. It took the process of deconstruction a step further. Taking the prototype of rearranged text, it was asked to look at the degree of overlap between similar rules originating from different chapters and to identify inconsistencies, discrepancies, or conflicts between these similar rules. The task force proposed revisions to increase consistency and prepared another prototype for a reorganized Part I.[10] The rearrangement of the text of the rules began a process of visualizing a new organization for the structure of the cataloging code.

The need for deconstruction was also supported from work coming out of the action item from the Toronto conference about the primacy of content over carrier. Rule 0.24 instructed catalogers to give primacy to the physical carrier, and to follow the rules for one class of materials:

> It is a cardinal principle of the use of part I that the description of a physical item should be based in the first instance on the chapter dealing with the class of materials to which that item belongs. In short, the starting point for description is the physical form of the item in hand, not the original or any previous form in which the work has been published.[11]

The ALCTS CCS Committee on Cataloging: Description and Access (CC:DA) was asked to examine 0.24 and prepare a rule revision proposal. The CC:DA task force identified two aspects of the problem: (1) how to describe a bibliographic resource that has multiple characteristics and (2) how to deal with identical intellectual content existing on a variety of carriers, also called the "format variation problem" in their report. They prepared a revision proposal that partially dealt with the first aspect and led to the amendment of rule 0.24 in 2001. The amendment instructed the cataloger to "bring out all aspects of the item being described, including its content, its carrier, its type of publication, its bibliographic relationships, and whether it is published or unpublished."[12] It eliminated the previous instruction to choose one aspect.

The revision did not indicate any precedence among the classes of materials, nor did it address the inconsistency in categorization of the classes of materials. The task force recognized that any changes to the class of materials concept would necessarily entail changes to the structure of Part I of AACR2. The task force clearly indicated that their proposed revision was an interim step because a full resolution of the problem would require an extensive reorganization of AACR2. They supported and encouraged the reorganization of Part I.[13]

In April 2004, the Committee of Principals (CoP) and the JSC decided that the degree of reorganization and changes required had surpassed the level of "amendments" and warranted a comprehensive revision of the rules. They named the new revision AACR3. The JSC endorsed the process of logical deconstruction. They also explicitly provided the new organizing framework with their intention to align the rules with the concepts and terminology used in the FRBR model.[14] A new draft of Part I was prepared. The proposed changes for AACR3 increased the integration of FRBR into the cataloging rules. The division into Parts I and II continued to mirror AACR2's structure, with the addition of a third part for authority control. But there was a new structure for the chapters within Part I. The draft also demonstrated a new approach to class of materials and general material designations, where there was a conscious differentiation between the type of content and the type of medium. The class of materials concept was in the process of being removed and replaced with a new, more logically rigorous and extensible framework for the technical and content description of resources.

As the new changes were proposed, tested, and discussed, it became evident that the standard was moving in the right direction, but it had not yet gone far enough.[14] In April 2005, the Committee of Principals and the Joint Steering Committee announced a further change in approach. Rather than trying to work within the AACR2 structure, the decision was made to abandon totally AACR2's structure and move to a more complete alignment with the FRBR model. The name of the standard was also changed to *Resource Description and Access*, to indicate the degree of change.

We can think of RDA as the product of a thorough deconstruction of AACR2 and a rebuilding into a new standard around the framework of the FRBR and FRAD conceptual models. During the collective deconstruction of Part I of AACR2, the individual rules were taken out of their chapters. They were removed from the "class of material" structure that defined Part I of AACR2. A few rules or instructions were eliminated, some were changed, some were generalized, and new ones were added. A large number of the AACR2 rules were reworded to fit with RDA's vocabulary and were placed in a new location within RDA's structure, but were essentially kept the same. RDA uses many of the old building blocks, and rearranges them in a new structure built on the theoretical framework expressed in the FRBR and FRAD conceptual models. Thus, there are recognizable links to AACR2, and there are RDA instructions that are simply reworked AACR2 rules, but the orientation of the standard as a whole has changed. In its alignment with the FRBR and FRAD conceptual models, RDA is built around a new, explicit, and logically sound theoretical framework.

NOTES

1. The Joint Steering Committee for Revision of AACR changed its name to the Joint Steering Committee for Development of RDA in 2007. When reference is made to the JSC, or the Joint Steering Committee, it refers to this committee, under its earlier or later name, depending on the context.

2. Joint Steering Committee for Development of RDA, "Issues Deferred until after the First Release of RDA" (5JSC/Sec/6/Rev; August 5, 2009), www.rda-jsc.org/docs/5sec6rev.pdf.

3. Anglo-American Cataloguing Rules, 2nd ed. (Chicago: American Library Association; Ottawa: Canadian Library Association, 1978), p. v.

4. Joint Steering Committee for Development of RDA, "Strategic Plan for RDA, 2005–2009" (5JSC/Strategic/1/Rev/2; November 1, 2007), www.rda-jsc.org/stratplan.html (last updated: July 1, 2009).

5. RDA 0.2.

6. JSC, "Strategic Plan."

7. The list of action items is a list of issues that urgently needed action. Joint Steering Committee for Revision of AACR, "International Conference on the Principles and Future Development of AACR: Action Items, Progress Report, July 2005," www.rda-jsc.org/intlconf2.html.

8. Tom Delsey, "The Logical Structure of the Anglo-American Cataloguing Rules" (1998), www.rda-jsc.org/docs.html#logical.

9. Ibid., part 1, recommendation no. 1.

10. ALCTS Committee on Cataloging: Description and Access, Task Force on Consistency across Part 1 of AACR, Documents, www.libraries.psu.edu/tas/jca/ccda/tf-con1.html.

11. Anglo-American Cataloguing Rules, 2nd ed., p. 8.

12. ALCTS Committee on Cataloging: Description and Access, Task Force on Rule 0.24, "Overview and Recommendations Concerning Revision of Rule 0.24" (4JSC/ALA/30; August 16, 1999), p. 3, www.libraries.psu.edu/tas/jca/ccda/docs/tf-024h.pdf.

13. Ibid., p. 5.

14. Joint Steering Committee for Revision of AACR, "AACR3. Part I. Constituency Review of December 2004 Draft" (5JSC/AACR3/I; December 17, 2004), p. 3, www.rda-jsc.org/docs/5aacr3-part1.pdf.

15. For example, see the responses of the Library of Congress and the British Library. Library of Congress, "AACR3. Part I. Constituency Review of December 2004 Draft: LC Response" (5JSC/AACR3/I/LC response; March 25, 2005), p. 1, www.rda-jsc.org/docs/5aacr3-part1-lcresp.pdf. British Library, "AACR3. Part I. Constituency Review of December 2004 Draft: British Library Response" (5JSC/AACR3/BL response; March 31, 2005), p. 1, www.rda-jsc.org/docs/5aacr3-part1-blresp.pdf.

5

WHERE DO WE SEE CHANGES?

The aim of this chapter is to give an overview of RDA by looking at actual RDA instructions, often in comparison with equivalent or similar AACR2 instructions. This chapter also introduces some of the RDA instructions that have a significant impact and signal a change in cataloging practice. Training documentation will provide comprehensive, step-by-step coverage of the ways in which RDA instructions differ from AACR2 rules. This chapter walks through key features to increase familiarity with RDA:

> Principles, Objectives, and Conceptual Models
>
> Focus on the User
>
> Extensible Framework for Describing All Types of Resources
>
> Mode of Issuance
>
> Data Elements
>
> Additional Elements
>
> Core Elements
>
> Take What You See
>
> Emphasizing Relationships

PRINCIPLES, OBJECTIVES, AND CONCEPTUAL MODELS

As noted in chapter 2, "RDA and the International Context," RDA is in step with the Statement of International Cataloguing Principles and is aligned with the FRBR family of conceptual models. The FRBR and FRAD models are evident throughout RDA, both in the way the instructions fit together and in the text of the instructions. The development of RDA was guided by the concepts that the models identify and also by a set of defined objectives and principles. These objectives and principles guided the design of RDA and the content of its instructions, and helped to maintain logical consistency and coherence throughout the standard. The objectives and principles are listed in the introduction to RDA (0.4) (see figure 5.1).[1]

- **0.4** <u>Objectives and Principles</u>
      <u>Governing Resource</u>
      <u>Description and Access</u>
   0.4.1 General
- **0.4.2** Objectives
   0.4.2.1 Responsiveness to
       User Needs
   0.4.2.2 Cost Efficiency
   0.4.2.3 Flexibility
   0.4.2.4 Continuity
- **0.4.3** Principles
   0.4.3.1 Differentiation
   0.4.3.2 Sufficiency
   0.4.3.3 Relationships
   0.4.3.4 Representation
   0.4.3.5 Accuracy
   0.4.3.6 Attribution
   0.4.3.7 Common Usage or
       Practice
   0.4.3.8 Uniformity

FIGURE 5.1

**Objectives and principles of RDA
(RDA Toolkit, June 2010)**

FOCUS ON THE USER

The very first objective for RDA is responsiveness to user needs (0.4.2.1). This is not an abstract consideration. It is realized in each section of RDA with specific functional objectives written for each section. Each section begins with a general chapter, and the functional objectives and principles for that section are immediately stated, as shown in figure 5.2.

The functional objectives relate the instructions of that section back to the user tasks. The functional objectives underline the relationship between the data recorded and the user task that the data is intended to support.

The functional objectives vary from section to section. Each section has its own functional objectives because the instructions in each section cover the recording of different kinds of data. The functional objectives match with the section.[2]

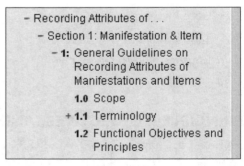

- Recording Attributes of . . .
   - Section 1: Manifestation & Item
      - **1:** General Guidelines on
          Recording Attributes of
          Manifestations and Items
          1.0 Scope
        + **1.1** Terminology
          1.2 Functional Objectives and
              Principles

FIGURE 5.2

Each section of RDA begins with a general chapter that includes section-specific functional objectives and principles (RDA Toolkit, June 2010).

For example, the functional objectives for Recording Attributes of Work and Expression (section 2), are as follows:

5.2 *Functional Objectives and Principles*

The data recorded to reflect the attributes of a work or expression should enable the user to:

a) *find* works and expressions that correspond to the user's stated search criteria

b) *identify* the work or expression represented by the data (i.e., confirm that the work or expression represented is the one sought, or distinguish between two or more works or expressions with the same or similar titles)

c) *understand* the relationship between the title used to represent the work and another title by which that work is known (e.g., a different language form of the title)

d) *understand* why a particular title has been recorded as a preferred or variant title

e) *select* a work or expression that is appropriate to the user's requirements with respect to form, intended audience, language, etc.

For Recording Relationships Between Works, Expressions, Manifestations and Items (section 8), they are:

24.2 *Functional Objectives and Principles*

The data recorded to reflect relationships between works, expressions, manifestations, and items should enable the user to:

a) find works, expressions, manifestations, and items that are related to those represented by the data retrieved in response to the user's search

b) understand the relationship between two or more works, expressions, manifestations, or items.

The functional objectives are a constant reminder of the importance of the relationship between the data and the user.

The text of RDA instructions also reflects this focus on the user. There are numerous instances in the instructions where there is leeway for cataloger judgment. There are instructions that include phrases such as "if . . . considered important for identification," or "if . . . considered important for access," or "if . . . considered to be important for identification or selection." The cataloger is given scope to make a judgment and guided in the judgment by reference back to user tasks.

For example,

2.3.1.6 *Introductory Words, Etc.*

Do not transcribe words that serve as an introduction and are not intended to be part of the title.

[examples]

Optional Addition

If the form in which the title appears on the source of information is considered to be important for identification or access, record that form of the title as a variant title.

The responsiveness to user needs is not an abstract idea confined to an introductory chapter, but is the recurring theme throughout all the text of RDA. RDA instructions provide practical guidance to record or create data that will support user tasks.

EXTENSIBLE FRAMEWORK FOR DESCRIBING ALL TYPES OF RESOURCES

One of the key goals for the development of RDA was to:

Provide a consistent, flexible, and extensible framework for both the technical and content description of all types of resources and all types of content.[3]

A major weakness of AACR2 was its inability to extend to the description of new kinds of publications. There were fundamental logical flaws that prevented flexibility and extensibility.[4] Taking the FRBR and FRAD models as the starting point, RDA introduces a new approach to the description of technical and content aspects of a resource. The models provide RDA with its underlying framework, and it is a logically defined framework. RDA's framework is not based on or shaped by a predefined set of content and carrier types. RDA's framework is based on the entities, attributes, and relationships that support the successful completion of user tasks. RDA then defines a set of data elements based on this framework. The data elements can be used in many different combinations. Data elements can be used in expected combinations for known resources and also in new combinations as new types of resources are created. The underlying framework permits flexibility and extensibility and maintains consistency by acting as the point of reference against which to test any future expansion of the data element set.

RDA also introduces a new approach to the categorization of technical and content aspects of a resource. RDA replaces the general material designations (GMDs) and the class of materials concept with a grid or framework that consists of three elements: content type, media type, and carrier type. The information that the GMDs communicated was useful information. The problem with the GMDs and with the class of materials concept was inconsistent categorization. The categories, used as terms in the GMDs and as class of material chapters, represented attributes at the level of work, expression, and manifestation. The GMD also intruded into the middle of the title statement, thus making it difficult to move beyond a single term.

Information about the type of content, media, and carrier is important for the user, whether as a means to discover resources, or to limit searches. RDA affirms the importance of this information for the user but takes a different approach than AACR2. The FRBR model identifies attributes associated with the work, expression, manifestation, and item entities. RDA builds on FRBR. Information that used to be conveyed through general and specific material designations is now rigorously sorted to distinguish between information about the expression and information about the manifestation. This information is recorded using a grid or framework consisting of three elements: content type, media type, and carrier type. This framework can provide a large number of combinations of data to cover both current and future types of resources.

Each of the three elements—content, media, and carrier types—has a set of controlled vocabulary. The vocabulary for all three elements was jointly developed by the Joint Steering Committee for Development of RDA, the RDA Editor, and developers of ONIX, a schema used by the publishing industry.[5] The terms were chosen as appropriate for the element, sufficiently differentiated one from another, and yet, together, they must cover all possible content and carrier types without leaving gaps. The terms are also at the same level of abstraction.

Content Type

Content type is an expression-level attribute. It is in the chapter on Identifying Works and Expressions. The definition of content type demonstrates the correlation with the FRBR entity *expression:*

> **6.9.1.1** *Scope*
> Content type is a categorization reflecting the fundamental form of communication in which the content is expressed and the human sense through which it is intended to be perceived. For content expressed in the form of an image or images, content type also reflects the number of spatial dimensions in which the content is intended to be perceived and the perceived presence or absence of movement.

RDA's definition of content type may seem a little philosophical, but it sets the scope for this element at a particular level of abstraction. For content type, the significant aspect is how the content is expressed and through which human sense the content is perceived. A difference in content type signals a different expression.

The terms used in content type capture the essence of the communication process:

cartographic dataset	cartographic tactile image
cartographic image	cartographic tactile three-dimensional form
cartographic moving image	cartographic three-dimensional form

computer dataset	tactile notated movement
computer program	tactile text
notated movement	tactile three-dimensional form
notated music	text
performed music	three-dimensional form
sounds	three-dimensional moving image
spoken word	two-dimensional moving image
still image	other
tactile image	unspecified
tactile notated music	

The FRBR model was used as a reference point against which to test the categories and develop a consistent set of terms, with all the terms at a similar level of abstraction. By adding "other" and "unspecified," RDA aims to cover all possible types so that something can always be recorded in this element. Content type is considered a core element, an element that should not be omitted, no matter how simplified the description.

Media Type

The definition of media type is very succinct:

3.2.1.1 *Scope*
Media type is a categorization reflecting the general type of intermediation device required to view, play, run, etc., the content of a resource.

It is an attribute of the carrier, and an attribute that distinguishes manifestations. The terms are at a lower level of abstraction compared to the terms used for content types.

The vocabulary used for media type are

audio	stereographic
computer	unmediated
microform	video
microscopic	other
projected	unspecified

Media type is not a core element, though recording it is encouraged because it allows for better data retrieval and data sorting. It is more challenging to retrieve when there is an absence of data, rather than when there is data present, even if it is data that may not seem to be needed by most users. The categories are not necessarily needed for display. For example, the term "unmediated" may be puzzling. Why record "unmediated"?

Media type functions as a part of a larger framework. These media type terms should be seen as categories within the larger framework of the three elements: content, media, and carrier types. It is the framework created through the three elements that allows for the full categorization of all types of resources, and also permits sorting and navigation through large retrieval sets, based on the controlled vocabulary used in these elements. Recording "unmediated" does not mean that we need to display the term "unmediated" to the user. But filling in all parts of the grid ensures consistency and completeness of data, and opens options for data display and data navigation. For example, the presence of a media type allows the user to locate a range of resources without needing to list specific carriers: a user with a visual impairment may only want resources whose media type is audio but may be able to use a range of different carriers. Using media type would permit the user to find all audio resources, regardless of the particular carrier.

Carrier Type

Carrier type is also a manifestation-level attribute. The definition of carrier type is closely intertwined with media type, but it is more concrete and specific than media type:

3.3.1.1 *Scope*

Carrier type is a categorization reflecting the format of the storage medium and housing of a carrier in combination with the type of intermediation device required to view, play, run, etc., the content of a resource.

Carrier types are closely correlated with media types and can be considered as the next level of granularity for the media types. Each carrier type corresponds to a single media type. Each media type encompasses several carrier types. If the carrier type is known, one could derive the media type.

The list of carrier type terms is subdivided in 3.3.1.3 according to media type:

Audio carriers
audio cartridge
audio cylinder
audio disc
audio roll
audiocassette
audiotape reel
sound-track reel

Computer carriers
computer card
computer chip cartridge
computer disc
computer disc cartridge
computer tape cartridge

computer tape cassette
computer tape reel
online resource

Microform carriers
aperture card
microfiche
microfiche cassette
microfilm cartridge
microfilm cassette
microfilm reel
microfilm roll
microfilm slip
microopaque

Microscopic carriers
microscope slide

Unmediated carriers
card
flipchart

Projected image carriers
film cartridge
film cassette
film reel
film roll
filmslip
filmstrip
filmstrip cartridge
overhead transparency
slide

object
roll
sheet
volume

Video carriers
video cartridge
videocassette
videodisc
videotape reel

Stereographic carriers
stereograph card
stereograph disc

other

unspecified

The list for the carrier types contains many familiar terms, terms that were used as specific material designations in AACR2. The element for carrier type is a separate element from the extent element. When using RDA, the cataloger is instructed to record a term as the carrier type, and the term is recorded using the precise vocabulary listed in 3.3.1.3. The terms are used in the singular, and with no further extensions or additions. The terms in the carrier type element are used as part of the framework for categorizing the type of resource, and all three elements use controlled vocabulary. It is the use of precise terms (or the possibility of using codes instead) that will enable precision in searching.

The carrier type is not the same as the attribute for extent. In AACR2, the specific material designations (SMDs) formed part of the statement of extent. Thus, the terms could appear in the singular or plural, and sometimes with additions, such as "ms." for manuscript. RDA uses two different elements: one for carrier type, using controlled vocabulary; and another element, extent, to record the extent, using carrier types when appropriate, in the singular or plural as applicable, and also offering the possibility of using other terms:

3.4.1.5 *Other Terms Used to Designate the Type of Unit*

Use a term in common usage (including a trade name, if applicable) to designate the type of unit:

a) if the carrier is in a newly developed format that is not yet covered in the list under 3.3.1.3

b) if none of the terms listed under 3.3.1.3 is appropriate

   or

c) as an alternative to a term listed under 3.3.1.3, if preferred by the agency preparing the description.

When recording data in the element for carrier type, there are strict guidelines; when recording data in the extent element, there is the possibility to use a broader range of terms.

When RDA instructs the cataloger to record the content, media, and carrier type, the instruction includes this sentence: "Record as many terms as are applicable to the resource being described." Then the cataloger is offered the alternative to record only the type that applies to the predominant part. The alternative permits continuity with practices already in place. But it is important to note that it is presented as an alternative, not as the main instruction. Where AACR2 forced the cataloger to choose a predominant part, RDA encourages the inclusion of as many types as are applicable. When cataloging a music CD, the resource will have one content type (performed music), but it is possible to record two media types (audio, computer) and two carrier types (audio disc and computer disc).

One might ask, How does one record metadata about technical and content aspects when the community may not have agreed what to call a new type of resource? It is important to remember that the cataloger is instructed to record data about the type of content, media, and carrier. RDA does not instruct on the use or display of this data. If the data is recorded, it can then be mapped to display in different ways. For example, if the data is recorded as content type = text, media type = unmediated, carrier type = volume, this could map to show the type of resource as "book." Or it could be mapped to display an icon of a book. Likewise, if the data recorded were content type = moving image, media type = video, carrier type = online resource, it could map to show the type of resource as "streaming video." Not all communities have to use the same labels. The terminology used to display the information can vary between different communities, so one community may want to take those three types and map it to display as "streaming video," and another to display it as "streaming media." A community could decide that only certain types or combination of types would display to the user. The types can also be mapped to a corresponding set of terminology in another language.[6] The underlying principle is consistency in recording the data and flexibility in displaying it. Another aspect of flexibility is the ease of making changes over time. We can map to a set of terminology and this terminology could be changed at a later date without changing the original data, just changing the mappings between the type and the display terminology. Tom Delsey made this point in the 2006 categorization document (5JSC/RDA/Part A/Categorization):

> Although the terms are designed to reflect common usage, it is recognized that usage varies from one community to another and changes over time. The terms used in the drafts should be treated simply as "labels" to designate the categories.
>
> . . . The instructions do not prescribe how the categories are to be displayed. The intent is to provide agencies using RDA flexibility to adapt displays to the needs and preferences of their user communities. Agencies may choose to be selective in which elements they display, and may display them either as separate elements

or in combination. They may also choose to display the categories using different terms than those that are listed. . . . The only requirement is that the elements be recorded so that they map directly to the categories as they are defined.[7]

The three elements of content, media, and carrier types bring a logically consistent approach to the description of content and carrier. There is a clear distinction between the content type and the media/carrier types. By having a framework, we can record data about a new type of resource even before the community has agreed upon a term to call it. When considering the terminology used and the possible redundancy of terms, it is important to remember that RDA is a content standard. Thus, it is important to record the data, and then there are many options for using or mapping this data. If someone has grave concerns about continuity with the previous general material designations, they could even map combinations of content, media, and carrier types back to the terminology used as GMDs.

MODE OF ISSUANCE

Mode of issuance is an attribute of the manifestation. It is a new data element in RDA that has no equivalent in AACR2. Mode of issuance is "a categorization reflecting whether a resource is issued in one or more parts, the way it is updated, and its intended termination" (2.13.1.1). It is an element that can be recorded in the description of every resource, and helps to identify the resource. The terms used in the mode of issuance element are: single unit, multipart monograph, serial, integrating resource. The instruction is to record as many terms as are applicable to the resource being described.

In addition to being a descriptive element, mode of issuance also continues to play a significant role in the whole description of the resource because it affects the choice of source of information to use as the basis of the description.

RDA instructions are not separated according to mode of issuance, whereas AACR2 had its separate chapter 12 for serials and integrating resources. RDA instructions are not separated according to content or carrier type, whereas AACR2 had separate chapters organized according to the class of materials. The basic assumption in RDA is that most instructions apply to all resources, and then there are additional instructions to apply for certain content types, certain carrier types, certain modes of issuance, etc. Mode of issuance is one more characteristic that needs to be taken into account when describing a resource.

DATA ELEMENTS

The term "element" is not new. It was used in AACR2. Though AACR2 and RDA both use the word "element," RDA's use of the term is different and moves closer to the meaning of element as part of a predefined element set used in a metadata schema. The editor, Tom Delsey, prepared a document showing the similarities between RDA's elements and metadata element sets:

RDA as a metadata element set

RDA can be viewed as a metadata element set (similar to the Dublin Core Metadata Element Set) insofar as it:

a) specifies a set of elements, element sub-types, and sub-elements that reflect the properties of a resource

b) defines each element, element sub-type, and sub-element

c) establishes parameters for the value representations recorded for each element, element sub-type, and sub-element.[8]

Recording data in defined, unambiguous elements is an important feature in RDA. It prepares the ground for use of RDA as a formally registered metadata element set that can operate in the Web environment.

The RDA elements correspond to the attributes and relationships that are identified and defined in the FRBR and FRAD models. RDA elements are independent, separate units of bibliographic or authority data. RDA moves away from the concatenation of different units of information into one long string of characters. Data is parsed into independent elements. The emphasis on data elements opens up the possibility of using any element as a search term or as a limit for a search. It also offers flexibility for the display of data.

Many of the data elements in RDA correspond to information that was recorded in AACR2, as shown in figure 5.3. However, AACR2 had less granularity in terms of recording the data. Different types of information were recorded in the same place. If we look at the AACR2 element "other physical details," part of the physical description area, there are many different units of information that can be recorded there, from information about illustrative content when describing a book, to details about base material, applied material, projection speed, track configuration, etc. It is difficult to use AACR2's "other physical details" as a fruitful way to improve searching because there are too many different types of information all recorded in the same place. RDA segments the data into separate data elements. Thus, when we look at chapter 3, "Describing Carriers," and chapter 4, "Describing Content," RDA includes a large set of data elements, each identified separately. As we will see later, in "Core Elements," this does not mean that all elements must be used all the time. The significance of data elements is that different kinds of data are recorded in appropriate elements, and these elements are unambiguously defined and identified.

When describing a resource, data about attributes and relationships are recorded and stored in separate, independent elements. Some of these elements are incorporated into access points. Currently, we are accustomed to the pre-set structure of access points. However, once data is recorded in separate RDA elements, it can be stored and displayed in different ways, opening up new possibilities. Thus, in the future, the pre-set structure of access points might disappear to be replaced with access points that are presented differently for different user communities, or are assembled "on the fly" in response

AACR2	RDA
all recorded as "other physical details"	*separately defined data elements*
(book) illustrative matter	illustrative content
(sound recording)	sound characteristic
	separate element sub-types[9]
type of recording	type of recording
playing speed	playing speed
groove characteristic (analog discs)	groove characteristic
track configuration (sound track films)	track configuration
number of tracks (tapes)	tape configuration
number of sound channels	configuration of playback channels
recording and reproduction characteristics	special playback characteristics
(motion picture/videorecording)	
aspect ratio	aspect ratio
& special projection characteristics	projection characteristic of motion picture film
sound characteristics	sound characteristic
colour	colour content
projection speed (motion pictures)	projection characteristic of motion picture film

FIGURE 5.3

Separate RDA elements correspond to information recorded as "other physical details" in AACR2.

to an actual query, with the presentation of data adjusted to respond to the nature of that query.

With clearly differentiated data elements, any element can potentially be used to initiate a search, to refine a search, to build displays, or to sort search sets. A search interface can take advantage of these clearly labeled and differentiated data elements in order to bring a higher level of precision to searches, and to organize results into meaningful displays. At the time of first implementation, RDA data will be encoded using MARC 21, and there will be some loss of granularity because many data elements will map back to one subfield, such as subfield b of the 300 field. Presentation of descriptive data and access points will also not change greatly. But, with clearly defined data elements, RDA opens the door to new ways to use and present this data.

ADDITIONAL ELEMENTS

As pointed out in the "Data Elements" section, RDA includes many new data elements (for an example, see the content of chapter 3, Describing Carriers, in figure 5.4). An important consideration was the granularity of data, so that data can be used and manipulated in different ways, using current or newly emerging technologies. Thus the process of breaking down long character strings, identifying types of data, and putting like data together in the same element has generated many new elements.

Chapter 7, "Describing Content," is another place where we are immediately aware of many additional elements. We can also see it in something as ordinary as recording a date. RDA has specific data elements for each type of date: publication date, production date, manufacture date, copyright date. Using AACR2, the data was recorded in a non-specific way. A human could interpret the data, but a machine could not, and thus the ability to use that data in automated processes was lost.

There are also new elements added to match the kind of information that is now considered essential but which never formed a part of AACR2, such as the inclusion of an element for the Uniform Resource Locator.

Some elements add greater precision to the data that is collected and better serve specific user populations. Taking the example of resources for those with a visual impairment, RDA includes data elements that record the description more precisely, and that, in the future, have the potential to improve searching. RDA considers the "tactile" dimension of a resource as an aspect of its content. A tactile resource is a different form of expression from an audiobook or a printed book. There are provisions for recording a full range of tactile content types, from cartographic tactile image to tactile music. The content type is then coupled with the media and carrier type to give more precise information. Tactile content is delivered on media and carrier types that are also used to deliver other content types. A braille book will have the content type "tactile

RDA	TOOLS	RESOURCES

- **3:** Describing Carriers
  - **3.0** Purpose and Scope
  - + **3.1** General Guidelines on Describing Carriers
  - + **3.2** Media Type
  - + **3.3** Carrier Type
  - + **3.4** Extent
  - + **3.5** Dimensions
  - + **3.6** Base Material
  - + **3.7** Applied Material
  - + **3.8** Mount
  - + **3.9** Production Method
  - + **3.10** Generation
  - + **3.11** Layout
  - + **3.12** Book Format
  - + **3.13** Font Size
  - + **3.14** Polarity
  - + **3.15** Reduction Ratio
  - + **3.16** Sound Characteristic
  - + **3.17** Projection Characteristic of Motion Picture Film
  - + **3.18** Video Characteristic
  - + **3.19** Digital File Characteristic
  - + **3.20** Equipment or System Requirement
  - + **3.21** Item-Specific Carrier Characteristic
  - + **3.22** Note

FIGURE 5.4

The table of contents for RDA chapter 3, "Describing Carriers," shows many examples of newly defined data elements (RDA Toolkit, June 2010).

text," media will be "unmediated," and the carrier will be "volume." Additional details are recorded in other data elements. RDA includes separate data elements for recording the production method for tactile resources (3.9.3.), and for the layout of tactile text (3.11.4). Since the content may be tactile music, there is also a data element to record the layout of tactile musical notation (3.11.3). There is another data element to record the form of tactile notation used to express the content, such as braille code, mathematics braille code, or tactile musical notation (7.13.4). Here, we can also record the level of contraction, such as uncontracted or grade 2, etc.

In the process of aligning RDA with the FRBR and FRAD conceptual models, many data elements were introduced to match the attributes and relationships mapped in the conceptual models. The example used earlier, in chapter 3, "FRBR and FRAD in RDA," was the addition of data elements to record all the attributes of person as identified in the FRBR and FRAD models.

9.	**Identifying Persons**
9.0	Purpose and Scope
9.1	General Guidelines on Identifying Persons
9.2	Name of the Person
9.3	Date Associated with the Person
9.4	Title of the Person
9.5	Fuller Form of Name
9.6	Other Designation Associated with the Person
9.7	Gender
9.8	Place of Birth
9.9	Place of Death
9.10	Country Associated with the Person
9.11	Place of Residence
9.12	Address of the Person
9.13	Affiliation
9.14	Language of the Person
9.15	Field of Activity of the Person
9.16	Profession or Occupation
9.17	Biographical Information
9.18	Identifier for the Person
9.19	Constructing Access Points to Represent Persons

The information recorded about person is much more than what is usually required to distinguish between two persons with the same name. Data about the person is not just the data required to formulate an authorized access point. It moves beyond what is required for an access point and toward a record for the person. An authority record for the person was beyond the scope of AACR2, but it is the current context for cataloging work in a MARC 21 environment. RDA introduces new bibliographic data elements, and also new authority data elements, with the aim of having unambiguous data in clearly defined data elements.

CORE ELEMENTS

RDA identifies a set of core elements. RDA does not identify "levels" of description. It also does not identify each element as mandatory or optional. RDA takes a different approach and identifies a set of elements that are considered to be the minimum set. These elements are the ones that contain data about the attributes and relationships that have the highest value in fulfilling user tasks. The decision about which elements are core is based on the FRBR and FRAD analyses that demonstrate how each attribute and relationship is used to complete user tasks. Core elements are a subset of data elements and cannot support all user tasks in the same way that the full set of RDA elements can. Instead subsets of essential tasks were identified:

0.6 *Core elements*

0.6.1 *General*

Certain elements in RDA are identified as core elements.

The RDA core elements for describing resources were selected from those that reflect attributes and relationships designated in FRBR as supporting the following user tasks:

identify and *select* a manifestation

identify works and expressions embodied in a manifestation

identify the creator or creators of a work.

The RDA core elements for describing entities associated with resources were selected from those that reflect attributes and relationships designated in FRAD as supporting the following user tasks:

find a person, family, or corporate body associated with a resource

identify a person, family, or corporate body

The set of core elements defines a base level, a level below which we should not drop because anything less will jeopardize the user's ability to fulfill any tasks. Once the core elements are identified, RDA then incorporates a fair amount of flexibility.

0.6.1

. . .

As a minimum, a resource description for a work, expression, manifestation, or item should include all the core elements that are applicable and readily ascertainable. The description should also include any additional elements that are required in a particular case to differentiate the resource from one or more other resources bearing similar identifying information.

. . .

The inclusion of other specific elements is discretionary. The agency responsible for creating the data may establish policies and guidelines on levels of description and authority control to be applied either generally or to specific categories of resources and other entities, or it may leave decisions on the level of detail to the discretion of the individual creating the data.

We can include additional elements either for a particular case or as an institutional policy. Thus, different institutions can have different policies. An institution with an exhaustive collection of prints and posters may want to include all relevant elements, such as base material, applied material, and production method, whereas a small library may find the core elements sufficient for their user population. This flexibility also opens the door to nonlibrary communities, such as archives, to determine their own policy for which elements to include in addition to the core set.

TAKE WHAT YOU SEE

The principle of representation is an important principle in the design of RDA instructions: The data describing a resource should reflect the resource's representation of itself (0.4.3.4). The principle is explained further, but it can be summarized in the phrase "Take what you see." This principle has an impact on the content of many instructions. By closely following the principle of representation, the process of describing a resource is simplified because there are fewer exceptions. It also opens the door to the possibility of automated data capture and data reuse, and to streamlined workflows.

For many descriptive data elements, transcription remains the cornerstone. In RDA, transcription often comes closer to the principle of taking exactly what you see than in AACR2. In this example, the instruction is basically identical, except that RDA omits the instruction to abbreviate:

AACR2

1.2B. *Edition Statement*

1.2B1. Transcribe the edition statement as found on the item. Use abbreviations as instructed in appendix B and numerals as instructed in appendix C.

RDA

2.5.1.4 *Recording Edition Statements*

Transcribe an edition statement as it appears on the source of information.

In AACR2, I transcribed the edition statement, but I also abbreviated (and made changes in how I recorded numerals). AACR2 combined transcription with the space limitations of the catalog card. Thus, I was not really taking what I saw. In RDA, if "3rd ed." is on the title page, I transcribe: 3rd ed.; if "Third edition" appears on the title page, I transcribe: Third edition. Similarly, when recording the name of the publisher using RDA, I record the name as found. I do not introduce abbreviations. If the name is abbreviated in the source of information, then it is recorded in the abbreviated form. If it appears in full, it is recorded in full.

Abbreviations were important in the era of card catalogs, when the information had to be recorded on a small rectangle of cardboard. In the current era of online catalogs, there is no longer a pressing need to limit the number of characters used to describe a resource. By removing these instructions, RDA follows the principle of representation more closely than AACR2.[10]

The instructions on recording inaccuracies or spelling mistakes in a title have also changed. In AACR2, the instruction was to transcribe the inaccuracy and supply the correction in the same place. In RDA, there is no equivalent to the general AACR2 rule 1.0F, to transcribe the inaccuracy and then add [sic] or i.e. and the correction in square brackets, or supply missing letters in square brackets. RDA 1.7.9 instructs me to transcribe the inaccuracy and, if considered important for identification or access, to make a note correcting the inaccuracy. With an inaccuracy in the title, I am instructed to record the corrected form as a variant title. Thus, RDA follows the principle of representation and then gives various means by which to ensure identification and access without disturbing the transcribed element.

On the source of information:		The wolrd of television
AACR2		The wolrd [sic] of television
	or	The wolrd [i.e. world] of television
RDA *Title proper*		The wolrd of television
RDA *Variant title*		The world of television

RDA does make one exception: in the case of serials and integrating resources. It maintains continuity with AACR2 and with the international serials cataloging community. RDA 2.3.1.4 instructs me to record the title as it appears, except as follows:

> **Inaccuracies.** When transcribing the title proper of a serial or integrating resource, correct obvious typographic errors, and make a note giving the title as it appears on the source of information . . . In case of doubt about whether the spelling of a word is incorrect, transcribe the spelling as found.

The principle of representation is also followed in the instructions on transcribing long titles and statements of responsibility. The main instruction is to transcribe exactly what appears on the source of information. The alternative is to omit information. The default is to follow the principle of representation fully. This close adherence to the principle of representation is especially obvious when looking at the differences in recording lengthy statements of responsibility:

AACR2

1.1F5. If a single statement of responsibility names more than three persons or corporate bodies performing the same function, or with the same degree of responsibility, omit all but the first of each group of such persons or bodies. Indicate the omission by the mark of omission (. . .) and add *et al.* (or its equivalent in a nonroman script) in square brackets.

RDA

2.4.1.5   *Statement Naming More Than One Person, Etc.*

Record a statement of responsibility naming more than one person, etc., as a single statement regardless of whether the persons, families, or corporate bodies named in it perform the same function or different functions.

In RDA, there are no restrictions about recording lengthy statements of responsibility. There is an alternative that maintains continuity with AACR2 1.1F5, but it is an alternative, not the main instruction:

2.4.1.5   *Optional Omission*

If a single statement of responsibility names more than three persons, families, or corporate bodies performing the same function, or with the same degree of responsibility, omit all but the first of each group of such persons, families, or bodies. Indicate the omission . . .

During the development of RDA, care was taken to develop a set of principles, informed by the International Cataloguing Principles, and to make sure that the instructions reflected these principles. Principles, such as the principle of representation, ensure a coherent set of instructions. By following the principle of representation, consistency is maintained between the data recorded and the data on the resource itself. The principle of representation simplifies the process of describing a resource by eliminating exceptions to transcription.

The principle of representation also allows for automated data capture, or reuse of data from other sources—for example, from a publisher, or from a digital object's metadata. RDA's instructions on transcription allow for some modifications, if it suits the needs of an agency and its user community. RDA also includes an alternative where there is absolutely no modification of the data:

Alternative at RDA 1.7.1:

If data are derived from a digital source of information using an automated scanning, copying, or downloading process (e.g., by harvesting embedded metadata or automatically generating metadata), transcribe the element as it appears on the source of information, without modification.

In this instruction, RDA moves to an absolute "take what you see" approach. As long as the original data is accurate, it can be accepted without changes. Energy can then be focused on adding additional elements that enhance the usability of the data, such as augmenting the description or constructing controlled access points.

EMPHASIZING RELATIONSHIPS

The FRBR and FRAD models are entity relationship models. Relationships are a key part of the models. The models emphasize the importance of relationships between entities and the role of relationships in the successful achievement of user tasks. RDA places great importance on relationships. Of the ten sections, six are devoted to recording relationships (see figure 5.5).

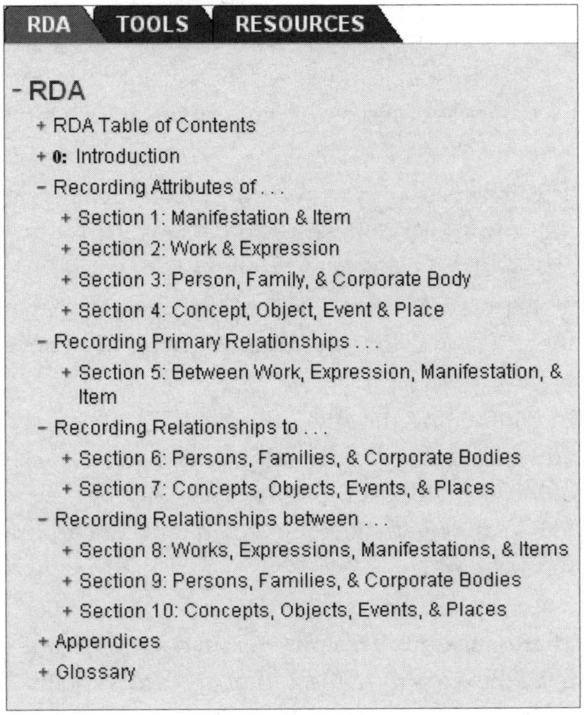

As mentioned earlier, Sections 4, 7, and 10 are essentially placeholders to allow a full mapping between the FRBR family of models and RDA. Even so, we can see the emphasis that RDA places on recording the full range of relationships associated with a resource, between re-

RDA   TOOLS   RESOURCES

- **RDA**
  + RDA Table of Contents
  + **0:** Introduction
  - Recording Attributes of . . .
     + Section 1: Manifestation & Item
     + Section 2: Work & Expression
     + Section 3: Person, Family, & Corporate Body
     + Section 4: Concept, Object, Event & Place
  - Recording Primary Relationships . . .
     + Section 5: Between Work, Expression, Manifestation, & Item
  - Recording Relationships to . . .
     + Section 6: Persons, Families, & Corporate Bodies
     + Section 7: Concepts, Objects, Events, & Places
  - Recording Relationships between . . .
     + Section 8: Works, Expressions, Manifestations, & Items
     + Section 9: Persons, Families, & Corporate Bodies
     + Section 10: Concepts, Objects, Events, & Places
  + Appendices
  + Glossary

FIGURE 5.5

Of the ten RDA sections, six are devoted to recording relationships (RDA Toolkit, June 2010).

sources, and between the entities responsible for resources. The instructions ensure that all types of relationships are recorded and well identified.

RDA also places no limits on the number of authorized access points. RDA eliminates the "rule of three" when describing the resource; it also eliminates this restriction when giving access to the resource. Chapter 21 of AACR2 had numerous rules that restricted the number of access points for collaborative works. For example,

From AACR2 21.7B1

If there are more than three works but only two or three persons or bodies responsible, make an added entry (or name-title added entry when appropriate) under the heading for each person or body.

Equivalent instructions are absent in RDA. Instead, RDA points to functional objectives when recording relationships between a resource and a person, family, or corporate body:

18.2. *Functional Objectives and Principles*

The data recorded to reflect relationships to persons, families, and corporate bodies associated with a resource should enable the user to *find* all resources associated with a particular person, family, or corporate body.

To ensure that the data created using RDA meet those functional objectives, the data should reflect all significant relationships between a resource and persons, families, and corporate bodies associated with that resource.

The instruction is to record all significant relationships. The examples in section 6, "Recording Relationships to Persons, Families, and Corporate Bodies Associated with a Resource," especially in chapters 19 (associated with a work) and 20 (associated with an expression), illustrate that there are no maximums. If using the core set of elements, then RDA specifies a minimum (18.3). RDA never limits the maximum.

In eliminating the rule of three, RDA even goes a step further. When constructing the authorized access point for a collaborative work, the main instruction is to take the name of the one with principal responsibility, or if there is no one with principal responsibility, to take the first named person, family, or corporate body, followed by the preferred title for the work.

There is also an alternative instruction that allows for the possibility of including the names of all the creators in the authorized access point. Applying the alternative instruction, the authorized access point is constructed using the names of all the creators followed by the preferred title for the work, as described in 6.27.1.3, "Collaborative Works":

Alternative at RDA 6.27.1.3

Include in the authorized access point representing the work the authorized access points for all creators named in resources embodying the work or in reference sources (in the order in which they are named in those sources), formulated according to the guidelines and instructions given under 9.19.1, 10.10.1, or 11.13.1, as applicable.

For example:

Gumbley, Warren, 1962– ; Johns, Dilys; Law, Garry. Management of wetland archaeological sites in New Zealand

Resource described: Management of wetland archaeological sites in New Zealand / Warren Gumbley, Dilys Johns, and Garry Law

This alternative does not reflect traditional library citation practices, and it may not be possible to encode it immediately. It does demonstrate the way RDA was designed to accommodate the practices of other metadata communities, in this case a practice of abstracting and indexing services.

RDA provides ways to record the nature of the relationship. Records created using AACR2 did include information about relationships, but the nature of the relationship usually had to be ascertained by reading the record. Precise information about relationships can potentially create useful pathways through large amounts of data, enabling a user to navigate successfully through large catalogs or databases; it can also potentially be used to improve the sorting, collocating, and display of search results. However, to use this information in an online environment, it is important to add consistent data about the nature of the relationship. Promoting the use of a controlled vocabulary means that this information is present, and it is present in a recognizable form, so that it can be picked up by automated processes and used for navigation and data display. RDA instructs us to record relationships and also to record an appropriate relationship designator. The relationship designators are a set of controlled vocabulary terms that indicate the nature of the relationship more precisely than the element used to record the relationship. For example, see the following from chapter 18, "General Guidelines on Recording Relationships to Persons, Families, and Corporate Bodies Associated with a Resource":

18.5.1.3. *Recording Relationship Designators*

Record one or more appropriate terms from the list in appendix I with an identifier and/or authorized access point representing the person, family, or corporate body to indicate the nature of the relationship more specifically than is indicated by the defined scope of the relationship element itself.

RDA includes three appendices of relationship designators (the fourth is included in the table of contents as a placeholder) (see figure 5.6). Appendices I, J, and K include lists of appropriate relationship designators and are organized according to FRBR entity to facilitate choosing the appropriate term. Appendices I and J list designators that are useful in mapping the relationships between resources and precisely identifying the relationship of responsibility between a person, family, or corporate body and a resource. Appendix K is particularly useful when working with authority data.

The designators listed in appendix I are intended to be recorded in conjunction with the access point for the person, family, or corporate body. If we look at the terms used in appendix I, there are the expected terms for the creator of a work, such as author, composer, or cartographer. There are also terms for other types of relationships to the work, such as production company or issuing body. There are designators at the expression level: persons, families, or corporate body who have contributed to the creation of an expression, such as abridger, editor, recording engineer, translator, transcriber, or performer. This last term, performer, can also be specified more narrowly as actor, commentator, narrator, speaker, or teacher. There are also persons, families, or corporate bodies whose contribution may be at the manifestation level, by having a role in manufacturing or publishing the manifestation: braille embosser, lithographer, or broadcaster. In addition, there are the item level relationship designators, such as former owner, illuminator, or inscriber.

```
 - Appendices
    + A: Capitalization
    + B: Abbreviations
    + C: Initial Articles
    + D: Record Syntaxes for Descriptive Data
    + E: Record Syntaxes for Access Point Control
    + F: Additional Instructions on Names of Persons
    + G: Titles of Nobility, Terms of Rank, Etc.
    + H: Dates in the Christian Calendar
    + I: Relationship Designators: Relationships between a
         Resource and Persons, Families, and Corporate
         Bodies Associated with the Resource
    + J: Relationship Designators: Relationships between
         Works, Expressions, Manifestations, and Items
    + K: Relationship Designators: Relationships between
         Persons, Families, and Corporate Bodies
    + L: Relationship Designators: Relationships Between
         Concepts, Objects, Events, and Places
```

FIGURE 5.6

**Relationship designator lists are provided
in the RDA appendices (RDA Toolkit, June 2010).**

The relationship designators in appendix J can be used in many ways, including in conjunction with access points. Most of the designators focus on the relationships between works and expressions. But there are also terms at the manifestation and item levels. The terms are organized both according to FRBR entities and according to the type of relationship: derivative, descriptive, whole-part, accompanying, or sequential. The terms are also given in two matching but different forms to indicate the direction of the relationship. Thus, I can record that work A is a "dramatization of" work B, and I can also record that work B has been "dramatized as" work A. The relationship designators often describe relationships that are currently noted in the body of a record, such as abridgment of, translation of, electronic reproduction of, digital transfer of, etc., possibly with or without additional controlled access points. The RDA relationship designators record the data in discrete, identified elements. The designators make the relationship visible and identify the relationship precisely; use of the designators means that the data is found in a consistent and identifiable location and can be used in automated processes for data navigation and data display. The designators can also be used simply to present information that the user can read.

In current catalogs, there is no clustering according to the type of relationship. One resource is somehow associated with another resource; a person, family, or corporate body is somehow associated with a resource. There is no way to discern the relationship without reading the record. Relationship designators add precise data about the nature of the relationship. This data can then be used to improve resource discovery. For example, a search on William Blake may return a set of results that includes resources where Blake is a creator, an illustrator, and perhaps also a former owner. The results are not usually sorted according to the type of relationship. By using relationship designators, the results can be clustered to show all the resources where Blake has a relationship of creator, then the resources where Blake has a relationship as illustrator, and then where Blake's relationship was that of a former owner. The use of controlled vocabulary means that automated processes can be programmed to pick up this vocabulary and cluster resources, possibly with the addition of labels, so that the user can quickly grasp the nature of the relationship and use this information to navigate, and to find, identify, and select relevant resources.

RDA introduces additional precision in the construction of authorized access points so that the access point can convey information about the nature of the relationship. The relationship designators are one way to make an authorized access point more precise. There are other additions as well.

RDA includes instructions for the construction of authorized access points to identify works and expressions. These instructions are found in chapter 6, "Identifying Works and Expressions." Chapter 25 in AACR2 did address access points for works, and also made some small and uneven attempts to identify expressions, in 25.5, "Additions to Uniform Titles." The FRBR model identifies the role of the expression entity and demonstrates that it is an important entity for the user. RDA includes instructions for the construction of authorized access points to represent both a work and a particular expression of a work. At 6.27.3, RDA instructs how to construct an authorized access point that represents an expression: extend the authorized access point for a work by adding, as applicable,

a) a term indicating content type (see 6.9)

b) the date of the expression (see 6.10)

c) a term indicating the language of the expression (see 6.11)

    and/or

d) a term indicating another distinguishing characteristic of the expression.

RDA includes a range of data that can be added to create the authorized access points fully identifying any expression. We can choose the data that makes the most sense for identification of a particular expression. One of the examples at 6.27.3 illustrates the use of language and content type:

Brunhoff, Jean de, 1899–1937. Babar en famille. English. Spoken word

Resource described: Babar and his children. *An audio recording of an English translation of the children's story*

This access point relays a lot of information to the user, such as the relationship of the resource to the original work, for example, indicating that it is a translation into

English, and giving the form of expression as spoken word. The authorized access point representing an expression is a very effective tool for the collocation of results. It brings together all the manifestations that embody the work, but it also organizes the result set according to the different expressions. Thus the results retrieved by the user, even without new advanced search interfaces, are clearly understandable and easily navigable.

RDA aims to reduce ambiguity and improve precision. An example is the avoidance of abbreviations when constructing authorized access points. For example, we will no longer use "b. 1789" or "d. 1852" in an authorized access point. We use the full word, "born 1789" or "died 1852" (9.19.1.3). Similarly, in an authorized access point for a manuscript or reproduction of a manuscript of a religious work, we add "manuscript" using the full word, not the abbreviation (6.30.4). Similarly, in authorized access points representing musical expressions, when it is an arrangement, we add the full word "arranged" (6.28.3.2), not the abbreviation.

Another example of the ways in which RDA aims for precision in access points is the decision to drop the use of the term *polyglot*. Polyglot was used in authorized access points to identify a resource that consisted of three or more expressions of the same work in different languages. Polyglot does not communicate useful information, because the languages are not identified, nor does it permit meaningful collocation or navigation. Instead, RDA instructs us to construct an authorized access point for each language expression.

SUMMARY

RDA has a theoretical framework as its foundation. The FRBR and FRAD conceptual models provide the underlying framework. This framework is further refined and augmented with a set of objectives and principles. RDA focuses on recording and constructing of data that will support the successful completion of the user tasks. This focus guides every part of RDA. RDA includes place for cataloger judgment because the theoretical framework not only shapes RDA but can also guide a cataloger's decisions. RDA instructions, using phrases such as "if . . . considered important for identification or access," leave the decision to the cataloger. The FRBR and FRAD models provide the theoretical framework to guide decisions when a circumstance is not explicitly covered in the instructions.

A key element of RDA was the development of a flexible and extensible framework to describe the content and technical aspects of any resource, whether a currently known resource or one that has yet to be produced. RDA also has a flexible and extensible framework or grid for the categorization of content type, media type, and carrier type. By using a grid consisting of the three terms, RDA builds in the possibility of many different combinations and provides a way to extend content and carrier categorizations to newly emerging types of resources. In addition to covering all content and technical aspects, RDA also covers all modes of issuance and does not segregate rules according to the mode of issuance. Most instructions in RDA are generally applicable to all resources, with additional instructions when required for certain content or carrier types or for certain modes of issuance.

RDA parses data into discrete data elements, making it possible to use this data in different ways, whether for display or for automated processing by machines. The data may have been recorded previously, but often it was embedded in long character strings or recorded in the same place as many other different types of data. RDA elements are identified with specific scopes; different kinds of data are separated into appropriate data elements. For this reason, RDA has many new data elements. It also has new data elements to cover bibliographic and authority data that was identified as important in the FRBR and FRAD models and may not have had a specific place in AACR2.

RDA identifies a set of core elements. The set of core elements are the minimum required. They form a baseline. The cataloger is encouraged to use additional elements if needed to ensure that a user will find, identify, select, and obtain the appropriate resource.

An important principle that has had an impact on the content of RDA instructions is the principle of representation. Adherence to this principle makes description easier by eliminating many exceptions. It also positions RDA as a standard that supports resource description in a digital world by allowing for data capture and reuse.

In its alignment with the FRBR and FRAD models, RDA's instructions are grouped into those that record attributes and those that record relationships. Relationships are essential for navigation and resource discovery. RDA places great importance on recording all types of relationships and on precisely identifying these relationships.

By improving the data that is recorded and the access points that are constructed, RDA sets the stage for improving the user experience of resource discovery, whether in traditional library environments or in Web environments.

NOTES

1. RDA objectives and principles are also on the JSC website: RDA, Resource Description and Access, Objectives and Principles (JSC/RDA/Objectives and Principles/Rev/3; July 1, 2009), www.rda-jsc.org/docs/5rda-objectivesrev3.pdf.

2. In chapter 3, "FRBR and FRAD in RDA," there are additional examples: the texts of the functional objectives for section 1, "Recording Attributes of Manifestation and Item," and Section 9, "Recording Relationships Between Person, Family and Corporate Body."

3. Joint Steering Committee for Development of RDA, "Strategic Plan for RDA, 2005–2009" (5JSC/Strategic/1/Rev/2; November 1, 2007), www.rda-jsc.org/stratplan.html (last updated: July 1, 2009).

4. See chapter 4, "Continuity with AACR2." See also Tom Delsey, "The Logical Structure of the Anglo-American Cataloguing Rules" (1998), www.rda-jsc.org/docs.html#logical; ALCTS

CC:DA Task Force on Rule 0.24, "Overview and Recommendations Concerning Revision of Rule 0.24" (4JSC/ALA/30; August 16, 1999), www.libraries.psu.edu/tas/jca/ccda/docs/tf-024h.pdf.

5. "RDA/ONIX Framework for Resource Categorization" (5JSC/Chair/10; August 3, 2006), www.rda-jsc.org/docs/5chair10.pdf.

6. For example, librarians from the Deutsche Nationalbibliothek have been experimenting with introducing multilingual vocabularies in the NSDL metadata registry, identifying German-language equivalents for content type vocabulary, mapping the terms to the English-language vocabulary, and presenting both terms as equivalent properties or terms to be used for the same concept. For example, notated music / schriftlich fixierte Musik at the NSDL Registry, http://metadataregistry.org/concept/show/id/519.html.

7. Tom Delsey, "Categorization of Content and Carrier" (5JSC/RDA/Part A/Categorization; August 4, 2006), pp. 3–4. www.rda-jsc.org/docs/5rda-parta-categorization.pdf.

8. Tom Delsey, "Encoding RDA Data" (5JSC/Editor/3; May 31, 2007), www.rda-jsc.org/docs/5editor3.pdf.

9. Sound characteristic has eight element subtypes. "Recording medium" is not in the list because it does not correspond to information recorded, according to AACR2, in other physical details. Using AACR2, information about the recording medium was recorded in a note.

10. On the subject of abbreviations, RDA also moves away from the use of abbreviations in elements that are not transcribed. In these cases, the change responds to the objective of being responsive to user needs. For example, when recording extent, common abbreviations such as p. and v. are no longer used. The full words—pages, volumes—are used instead. Likewise, Latin abbreviations are no longer used. Latin abbreviations, such as S.l., s.n., and et al. were used to supply information to the user, but they are no longer universally understood. RDA instructs the cataloger to supply a short descriptive phrase, such as "place of publication not identified" and "publisher not identified." These phrases are given in English, but the understanding is that the agencies that operate in other languages and scripts will find equivalent terms in the languages and scripts that they prefer (0.11.2).

6

IMPLEMENTING RDA: TRANSITION FROM AACR2 TO RDA

This chapter looks at some aspects of implementation, focusing particularly on the transition between AACR2 and RDA. RDA is a new standard, and there are fundamental differences between RDA and its predecessor. There are many aspects to learn, and training is an obvious part of the transition. As with all major changes in the cataloging environment, national libraries, library associations, and national cataloging committees will work together to plan, produce, and share training resources. Leaving aside the details of training, this chapter focuses on three factors that play a role in supporting a smooth transition:

1. **RDA Toolkit**

   RDA is released as part of an online tool called the RDA Toolkit. The Toolkit contains the full content of the standard, and it also contains additional documents and functionality. As a Web tool, RDA calls for new ways of working with the standard, but it also offers ways to make it easier to achieve the change.

2. **Encoding and display of RDA data**

   At the point of implementation of the first release, encoding and displaying RDA data is quite similar to encoding and displaying AACR2 data. Though there are some changes in the content of the data, the pieces are already in place to enable a continuation of encoding and display practices.

3. **Coordinated implementation**

   In 2007, the national libraries of Australia, Canada, Great Britain, and the United States published an announcement that they would work together to coordinate implementation, and they reaffirmed this intention in 2009. Development of RDA was an international initiative; implementation is also a collective activity that crosses national boundaries. Implementation is made easier through the coordination of decisions and the sharing of training documentation at the national library level.

RDA TOOLKIT

RDA was designed "for the digital world." It was designed as a standard to describe digital resources, as well as traditional resources; its data was designed to be efficient and usable in an online networked environment, and it was also designed to be used as an online tool.[1] The content of RDA is released as part of an online tool called the RDA Toolkit.[2] The RDA Toolkit consists of documents and software. The most important document is the full text of RDA. The Toolkit also contains related documents, such as the full text of AACR2, and documents outlining the RDA model and element set, such as the Entity Relationship Diagram (ERD). There are several different ways to navigate or search the Toolkit, as well as ways to change the display. The Toolkit includes workflows and mappings, features that support the integration of RDA into daily work. There is also scope for the creation and inclusion of customized files and documents. Making the transition to RDA entails learning the content of the standard and learning to use the new Web tool. But the added functionality of the Web tool makes the transition easier.

It is difficult to give a full sense of the scope and potential of a Web tool from a textual description. This section outlines some of the key features of the Toolkit, looking at them especially from the perspective of changing to RDA.

The Toolkit is divided into three sections. When I log in, there are three tabs in the navigation pane on the left side of the screen: RDA, Tools, and Resources.

RDA Tab

The RDA tab (see figure 6.1) includes the full text of RDA. The RDA text on this tab is the content of the standard as approved by the Joint Steering Committee. From the RDA tab, I can navigate through the content of RDA using the table of contents (see figure 6.2). In the navigation pane, the table of contents opens down

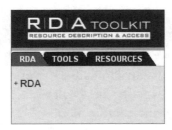

FIGURE 6.1

The RDA tab within the RDA Toolkit (June 2010)

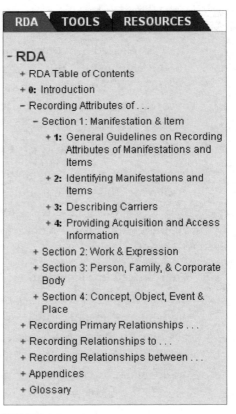

FIGURE 6.2

The RDA table of contents as displayed within the RDA Toolkit (June 2010)

to the detailed level of each numbered instruction, allowing me to go directly to the needed instruction. I click on the instruction and the text appears in the document pane. References within the text of RDA are active links, whether the reference is to another instruction in the same chapter or in a different section, or to a term in the glossary.

The content of RDA can also be filtered to present different views. The options are in the View Text menu. I can choose to hide examples. In some instructions, there are large sets of examples. If I want to see just the text of the instruction, to get an overview of the complete instruction, I can choose to filter out the examples. As soon as I choose a filtered view, this icon appears:

The icon reminds me that I am not seeing the full text of RDA; I am seeing a view from which some content has been subtracted.

RDA identifies a set of core elements. Section 0.6 of the standard contains a detailed explanation of all the core elements. Core elements are identified in the full text of the instructions with a label and, when needed, with explanations that derive from the information in 0.6. For example, some elements are core only if certain conditions apply; in other cases, only some subelements are required. An instance of this occurs in 2.5, "Edition Statement":

2.5 *Edition Statement*

Core Element

Designation of edition and designation of a named revision of an edition are core elements. Other sub-elements of edition statements are optional.

In search results and other places in the Toolkit, the cataloger is alerted about core elements through the core icon:

It is possible to choose a filtered view of the content of RDA, showing only instructions that pertain to the core elements. In this case, both the filtered and the core icons remain visible at the head of the screen while the filtering is in effect.

The filtered views are shortcuts. They remove parts of the standard, allowing the cataloger to see a streamlined version of the text. Since the filters subtract content, the Toolkit is designed to keep the cataloger constantly aware that they are viewing incomplete content.

Integrating the use of a new standard into daily work often entails a certain amount of marking text and adding annotations, explanations, etc. The Toolkit includes this functionality with the bookmarks feature. Bookmarks are not just placeholders but can also include lengthy annotations. They can be added, edited, or deleted using the Bookmark menu. They can also be hidden or displayed.

All documents in the Toolkit are searchable. There are two search options, located as part of the header pane: "quick search" and "advanced search." In the advanced search, I can limit the search in a number of ways, such as limiting it to RDA itself, or to certain sections and chapters of RDA, or limiting to instructions that apply specifically to a particular content type, media type, mode of issuance, or for a particular type of description (analytical, comprehensive, hierarchical), or limited to core elements only, etc. When the RDA search screen shows the options for limiting a search, each limit has a controlled list of terms displayed in a menu.

Content Type

General Only

Cartographic Only

Movement Only

Moving Images Only

Music Only

Still Images Only

Tactile Only

Text Only

Three-Dimensional Forms Only

For example, I can limit a search by a term for content type, such as Cartographic Only, or limit by a term for mode of issuance, such as Integrating Resources Only. These searches return all instructions relevant to that content type or mode of issuance. The terms are familiar because they come from the vocabulary used in RDA elements, but these searches are not simple keyword searches of the instructions. These searches use metadata embedded in the RDA instructions.

There is also a special search feature where I can search the text of RDA using an AACR2 rule number. This search feature is built on the mapping between AACR2 rules and equivalent RDA instructions. The third tab, Resources, which will be discussed in more detail below, includes the full text of AACR2. The presence of AACR2 in the Toolkit gives us an easy way to compare the text of AACR2 rules with RDA instructions. The results of a search using the AACR2 rule number may show a single result or a series of results depending on the ways in which the original rule was been moved, transformed, and reworded in RDA. Some AACR2 rule searches will not work because there has been a major change in approach, so there is no possibility of mapping between AACR2 and RDA This is the case, for example, for rules related to the general material designations.

Results for all searches are presented in weighted relevancy order. When there are multiple hits within a single chapter, I'm offered the choice of seeing these results in relevancy order, or in the order in which they appear in the chapter. Given that RDA instructions are organized from the general to the specific, many times it may be useful to read the instructions in the order in which they appear in the chapter.

Tools Tab

The Tools tab (see figure 6.3) offers ways to view and use the content of RDA, as well as practical tools to integrate the new standard into daily work. This tab was created with the front-line cataloger in mind.

The Element Set View and the Entity Relationship Diagram are two different ways to view an outline of RDA content.

The Element Set View is like a dictionary of RDA elements. Every RDA element is listed and includes the name of the element; its definition; the controlled vocabulary used in the element, when this is applicable; a list of instructions for recording data in this element and links to the full text of these instructions; and how to encode this data in MARC 21 and links to full information about encoding at the MARC 21 website. The instructions are not necessarily in numerical order, but in the order in which they will be most useful to a frontline cataloger. This summary view gives the cataloger a quick reference tool.

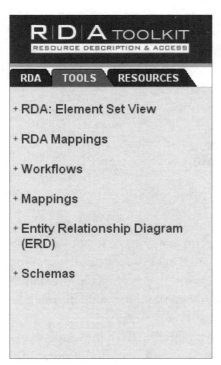

FIGURE 6.3

In addition to the RDA standard, several tools are included in the RDA Toolkit (June 2010).

The Entity Relationship Diagram (ERD) is one large diagram that has been broken into a series of diagrams to make it easier to view. The ERD presents a visual mapping of RDA elements. The diagrams are organized according to entity. There are diagrams to map the attributes of the entity and diagrams to map relationships. The diagrams can be used as a way to orient oneself to the underlying structure of RDA. They give an overview of the whole standard, showing all the elements and all the vocabulary used in elements that have controlled vocabulary. The diagrams are an outline of RDA's structure, without the text of any instructions, without principles, objectives, or explanations, etc. But they are precise diagrams of the structure and so are very detailed. Figure 6.4 shows an example of an ERD—Core Attributes of the Expression.

The diagrams also demonstrate the alignment with the FRBR and FRAD models. The diagrams of the attributes include references to the attributes in the FRBR and FRAD models,

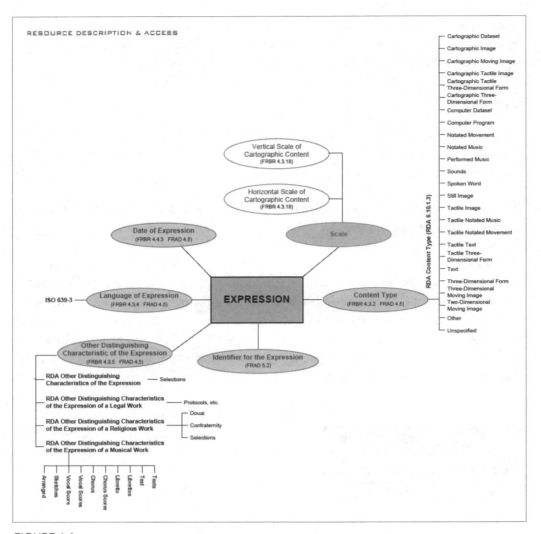

FIGURE 6.4

The RDA entity relationship diagram for the core atttributes of the expression, as shown in the RDA Toolkit (June 2010)

making it easy to see the closeness of the alignment. The diagrams of relationships do not include references to the models, but the relationships themselves closely echo the relationships in the FRBR and FRAD models. The diagrams give a visual representation of the content and structure of RDA, and also confirm RDA's alignment with the models.

Workflows and mappings are two important tools for integrating RDA into daily work. RDA is a thorough and detailed standard. Not everyone will need to become fully knowledgeable about all aspects of RDA. The workflows and mappings are practical procedure documents that provide pathways through RDA. They provide a way to start becoming acquainted with the text of RDA without being overwhelmed by the breadth of the full standard.

The workflow is a step-by-step procedure document. A workflow is written for one specific task or for one procedure in the process of describing resources and giving access to them. For example, there can be workflows for describing a particular type of resource, for recording authority data about a person or family or corporate body, or for carrying out an activity, such as transcription. The workflow pulls out all the instructions that are relevant to the task and organizes them into one step-by-step procedure. The workflow also reminds the cataloger of the decisions that are required, decisions about the type of description, decisions about options, etc. The workflow does not include the full text of the instructions, but it includes references to the instructions, which, in a Web environment, are live links into the full text of RDA. Workflows are a way to introduce staff to the content of RDA. They provide an opportunity to start applying RDA in practical, daily work before having a full, comprehensive knowledge of all parts of the standard. Workflows can be used to train staff and then, after training, to maintain consistency and efficiency with a uniform procedure document.

Workflows can also be customized by individual institutions to incorporate local decisions about options or local practices. The Tools tab gives access to existing workflows and also to the wizard for creating new workflows. An institution can begin by copying an existing workflow and editing it for their additional local needs. A library does not need to maintain local documentation at a separate location, but can integrate local policies and practices into customized workflow documents and store them as part of their profile within the Toolkit website.

Workflows are documents that can also be shared. When the Joint Steering Committee introduced the first workflows in 2008, as part of the documentation accompanying the RDA draft, their thought was that these documents would be devised by individuals or institutions and shared.[3] Workflows for general tasks could be shared among the cataloging community, eliminating the need for duplication of effort and possibly also encouraging a uniform application of RDA. The workflow can also be seen as a useful tool for specialized cataloging communities. Communities that currently prepare and maintain specialized manuals, such as the cartographic or rare materials cataloging communities, may choose to devise workflows for special types of content or carriers and share them as a way to support consistency and standardization within their community.

A mapping document is another practical tool that provides a pathway into the text of RDA and enables the cataloger to move quickly into cataloging with RDA. A mapping document demonstrates how to encode RDA data. It shows the correspondence between RDA elements and the elements, fields, and syntax of a particular encoding schema. The mappings can document the relationship between RDA and the encoding schema in either direction: mappings can start with RDA elements and show how and where the RDA data is encoded; mappings can also start with the units or syntax of the encoding schema and map to RDA elements.

As pointed out before, RDA is a content standard and is not tied to a single encoding schema. So it is possible to map to several encoding schema. The current, predominant encoding system used in libraries is MARC 21. Mappings between RDA and MARC 21 were first created during the development process, to demonstrate that RDA data could easily be encoded using MARC 21. Some changes to MARC 21 were also introduced to better accommodate RDA data.[4] The Tools tab mappings between RDA and MARC 21 are more detailed than those included in appendices D and E and include newly approved MARC 21 fields and fixed field values. Figure 6.5 is an excerpt from the mapping of RDA elements to MARC 21 authority fields and subfields.

9.2 RDA	Name of the Person			
9.2.2 RDA	Preferred Name for the Person	100, 400, 500 1st indicator 0 or 1	a	Personal name
9.2.2 RDA	Preferred Name for the Person	100, 400, 500 1st indicator 0 or 1	b	Numeration
9.2.3 RDA	Variant Name for the Person	400 1st indicator 0 or 1	a	Personal name
9.2.3 RDA	Variant Name for the Person	400 1st indicator 0 or 1	b	Numeration
9.3 RDA	Date Associated with the Person			
9.3 RDA	Date Associated with the Person	100, 400, 500 1st indicator 0 or 1	d	Dates associated with a name

FIGURE 6.5

An excerpt from the mapping of RDA elements to MARC 21 authority fields and subfields, provided in the RDA Toolkit (June 2010)

Like the workflows, the mappings do not include the full text of RDA instructions. They refer to the relevant RDA element, and the full text of the instructions for that element is one click away. The mappings also link to encoding information at the MARC 21 website. In some cases, there are one-to-one correspondences between MARC 21 subfields and RDA elements. When there is not a one-to-one correspondence—when MARC 21 is less granular than RDA—a range of RDA elements map to the subfield where they are encoded. The RDA Toolkit contains mappings between RDA elements and the MARC 21 fields and subfields used in both the authority and bibliographic formats.

The mapping between RDA and the MODS metadata schema is also available. Like the MARC 21 mapping, where MODS is less granular than RDA, several RDA elements map to the same MODS element. New mappings between RDA and other encoding schema will be added as they are developed.

Customized mappings can also be created, either starting from scratch or copying and editing an existing mapping. An institution might have a digital repository that uses its own encoding schema, or an institution may need to incorporate added details about local practices for their library management system. The aim is to have a mapping that can be used as a daily tool by staff. The ability to customize enables the efficient integration of local and standard documentation. An institution does not need to create and store local documentation separately, but can have its customized version of a mapping created and stored in the Toolkit, readily accessible alongside standard mappings and other cataloging tools. By creating local documentation in the Toolkit, the documents do not quickly become out of date, but are linked to the latest text of the instructions.

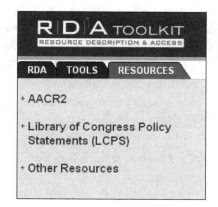

FIGURE 6.6

Additional resources are also included as part of the RDA Toolkit (June 2010).

The Tools tab also includes a feature called Schemas. Here is evidence of new ways to work with RDA data in a Web environment. At the time of first release and implementation of RDA, MARC 21 is the dominant encoding standard in the library world, and RDA data will be encoded using MARC 21. MARC 21 has a data structure that makes it difficult to exchange data with non-MARC 21 encoding environments. One of the aims of RDA is to make library data visible and usable in the Web environment. XML is an example of an open, flexible encoding schema that can support the exchange of data between different encoding environments. The XML schema is like a template that can then be completed by adding specific data, such as the title of the resource, date of publication, etc. Opening up and completing an XML schema simply requires the use of an XML editor, as opposed to the precise and narrow environment where MARC 21 records can be created. On the Tools tab, the section called Schema allows me to download a set of RDA elements as an XML Schema Definition (XSD). The schema is then used to create a XML document that describes the resource. The XML document is similar to a MARC 21 record except that it is encoded in such a way that its data can be used and exchanged more easily in a range of encoding environments. Thus, RDA data can be exchanged in the traditional MARC 21 format, but it is also ready to be used in new environments.

The third tab, Resources (figure 6.6), includes related documents and links to related documents or websites. The full text of AACR2 is available through this tab, and it can be accessed by browsing the table of contents. In the text of AACR2, there are also blue RDA icons:

This icon appears in the text of AACR2 when there are close equivalences between AACR2 rules and RDA instructions, and links to the RDA text. There is an underlying mapping between AACR2 rules and equivalent RDA instructions. This mapping supports the AACR2 rule number search (mentioned earlier) as well as these links from the text of AACR2 to the text of RDA.

If the AACR2 rule number maps to a single RDA instruction, clicking on the RDA icon takes me to the instruction in RDA. If the AACR2 rule number maps to several RDA instructions, clicking on the RDA icon takes me to a screen of search results. Some AACR2 rules will not have an icon because either the rule has no equivalent in RDA or there has beensuch a transformative change that it is not possible to map equivalences.

During the transition from AACR2 to RDA, different people will learn the new standard in different ways. Some will want to immerse themselves totally in the new standard, and learn it as a coherent whole, without reference to AACR2. Some will find it useful to move between the old and new standards, comparing texts, comparing wording, comparing structure, noting the changes and differences. The Toolkit has the functionality to support learning through the comparison of old and new. I can use the AACR2 rule number search or the RDA icons in the AACR2 text as ways to trace where a rule went. I can also open RDA on the RDA tab, and AACR2 on the Resources tab, and move back and forth between the tabs.

The Resources tab also includes links to documents and websites that contain information relevant to the use of RDA. Thus, there are links to the FRBR and FRAD models, to the MARC and Dublin Core websites, and to related initiatives, such as registering RDA element sets and RDA vocabularies so that they can be used in the semantic Web environment. The Resources tab can expand to include new relevant documents and links.

The Toolkit includes links from inside the Toolkit to relevant external resources, such as the links from the Element Set View to the corresponding encoding information at the MARC 21 website. When the Toolkit links to external resources, they are open access, Web-based resources. There are also links from subscription-based products into the Toolkit. Cataloger's Desktop links into the Toolkit. For example, when search results in Cataloger's Desktop include references to RDA, I can start from a Desktop search and, with a subscription to both, move right into RDA content in the Toolkit. Before the library community moves into an XML schema environment, an important link is the one between MARC based library systems and the Toolkit. The point of contact will be the Element Set View. Integrated library systems and cataloging services, such as Connexion, will link to RDA by going to the Element Set View.

Preparation for implementation will include training sessions on navigating through RDA and using the Toolkit. However, even at a summary level, one can see how the Toolkit provides several ways to view, learn, and use the content of RDA. There are different views of the content, such as the view that filters to show only core elements. The Toolkit includes a quick reference summary of RDA in the Element Set View, which is like a data dictionary. There is a visual presentation of the structure of RDA in the entity relationship diagram (ERD). There are different ways to search the contents of the Toolkit and to limit or expand searches. The Toolkit includes practical tools: the workflows and mappings. These tools provide easily accessible pathways into the content of RDA, starting from a specific task in the workflow document, or from a specific subfield or element in the mapping documents. To facilitate the transition, the full text of AACR2 is present in the Toolkit so that comparisons can easily be made. The Toolkit can be customized, from simple additions such as bookmarks and annotations, to the creation of local versions of workflows and mappings that integrate local decisions and practice. Training becomes easier because all documents are integrated in one site and are kept up to date as the standard is updated. The Toolkit offers a range of different ways to approach the content of RDA, so that we can start applying the new standard efficiently.

ENCODING AND DISPLAY OF RDA DATA

Changing to RDA is like switching railroad tracks. The track on which we began in the print-based world of the last century does not let us take full advantage of the new digital environment. The track is coming to its end. We still want to head in the same general direction, but we need to switch to the new track that so that we can keep moving forward. At the point where we switch, the similarities between the two tracks are important because they create the conditions where it is possible to change tracks in a fairly seamless manner. The differences will become increasingly apparent as we travel along the new track.

As we take a step forward, we also have to look backward and ensure that we do not lose the use of our legacy data. At the point of implementation, the intention is to make the transition to RDA as smooth as possible. Care has been taken to ensure that RDA and AACR2 records can interfile in the same catalogs. It is possible to encode RDA data with MARC 21 and to retain the same display of bibliographic data.

RDA is a content standard. The body of RDA consists of instructions about recording data. Encoding and presentation of data are mentioned only in the appendices.

> Appendix D—Record Syntaxes for Descriptive Data
>
> Appendix E—Record Syntaxes for Access Point Control

The two appendices provide practical guidance about using RDA data because the data needs to be encoded and it needs to be displayed. The appendices are the starting point for the mapping documents that are included in the Toolkit. Thus, even though RDA is silent on encoding and display, the appendices demonstrate a way to use the data in the existing context.

The scope of appendix D is to provide "guidelines on the presentation of data in accordance with ISBD specifications, and a mapping of the variable fields and subfields defined in the *MARC 21 format for bibliographic data* to the corresponding elements in RDA" (D.0). The scope of appendix E is similar: "This appendix provides guidelines on the presentation of access points and references derived from AACR2 rules and examples, and a mapping of the variable fields and subfields defined in the *MARC 21 format for authority data* to the corresponding elements in RDA" (E.0). Like the train moving from one track to another, it is important to maintain similarities between the tracks so that the transition happens smoothly and so that legacy data can coexist in the same databases with new RDA data.

To prepare for the transition, some adjustments to MARC 21 were needed to accommodate the encoding of RDA data.[5] The RDA/MARC Working Group was formed to identify the changes required to encode RDA data using MARC 21. The Working Group prioritized the areas requiring changes, beginning with those that were most urgently needed. Many RDA elements could fit within existing MARC 21 fields and subfields and fixed field values, even if it was not the ideal encoding situation. Given the need to balance the cost of change with the benefit of new content designation, some MARC 21 fields were left as they were.

RDA precisely defines elements and parses data into independent elements to prevent ambiguity and support machine processing. One example of a MARC 21 field that was segmented to make the data more usable is field 502, Dissertation Note. New subfields were added. Instead of one long character string that gives information about the type of degree, the granting institution, and the date that the degree was granted, now this information may be segmented into separate subfields. The new subfields correspond to RDA elements for the description of dissertations and theses:

RDA 7.9.2	Academic degree	MARC 21 502 $b
RDA 7.9.3	Granting institution or faculty	MARC 21 502 $c
RDA 7.9.4	Year degree granted	MARC 21 502 $d

The addition of the new subfields means that this data no longer has to be delivered as one long string, but can be segmented and made available as a way to search, to limit searches, to create displays, and for use in other machine processing.

In some cases, the data might not be encoded in a way that supports optimal use of the data, but there is a consistent place to record the data. RDA adds many new elements so that data is never recorded in an ambiguous element that is used for many different types of data. In preparation for the initial implementation of RDA, MARC 21 did not expand to include all RDA elements. For example, 300 subfield b will continue to be the place to record a range of different types of data. Fourteen different RDA elements map to this single subfield. Multiple RDA elements mapping to the same subfield will postpone the time when this RDA data can be used effectively, but, at least, it is recorded in one consistent place.

Certain critically important changes had to be made for day one of implementation, the most notable being the introduction of three new fields (336, 337, 338) to record three RDA elements—content type, media type, and carrier type. The three RDA elements replace the general material designation that was recorded in subfield h of the 245. In the new fields, information about content, media, and carrier can be recorded using the full word or phrase, as specified in RDA's instructions (RDA 6.9, 3.2, and 3.3), or using an equivalent shorthand code. The field includes a subfield to identify the source of the term or code. The fields were introduced to accommodate RDA data, but could also be used to record terms from other sources.

As part of the changes to accommodate RDA's approach to content and carrier, the list of values for fixed fields in the 007 and 008 were expanded. In some cases, RDA data maps to a "rough equivalent," but the aim is achieved of ensuring that RDA data maps to MARC 21. The expansion of fixed field values accommodates the categories that are used in RDA elements such as extent of still images (007/01), extent of notated music (008/20), base material (007/04), etc.

One of the key differences between RDA and AACR2 was the extent of authority data. RDA aligns with both FRBR and FRAD. The alignment with FRAD means that RDA includes many new elements pertaining to authority data. To accommodate the RDA authority data elements, MARC 21 includes new fields in the authority format. Examples of new fields to record attributes of a name include

field of activity	RDA 9.15 (person) and RDA 11.9 (corporate body)	MARC 21 372
gender	RDA 9.7	MARC 21 375
associated language	RDA 9.14 and 11.7	MARC 21 377

Examples of new fields in the authority and bibliographic format to record more precisely the attributes of a work or expression include

form of work	RDA 6.3	MARC 21 380
other distinguishing characteristics of work or expression	RDA 6.12	MARC 21 381

Content type is a new field defined for use in the bibliographic format and can also be used in the authority format because it carries information about an attribute of a work or expression. In our current database structures, where we use bibliographic and authority records, this data is relevant in both types of records because data about works and expressions is present in both records.

RDA places great emphasis on the recording of relationships and on the precise identification of the type of relationship. MARC 21 already contained a certain number of fields and subfields to record information about relationships, but not always identifying the precise nature of the relationships. MARC 21 was expanded to cover more precise identification, such as the expansion of relator terms and the addition of subfields i and 4 to fields recording relationships. Subfield i carries information about the relationship when the MARC tag or indicators are not specific enough. Subfield 4 carries the same information using codes.

This example shows the use of subfield i in tag 700 in the MARC 21 Format for Bibliographic Data:[6]

245 00 $a Alice in Wonderland, or, What's a nice kid like you doing in a place like this? / $c Hanna-Barbera Productions.

700 1 $i parody of (work) $a Carroll, Lewis, $d 1832-1898. $t Alice's adventures in Wonderland.

And here is an example of the use of subfield i in MARC tag 500 in the MARC 21 Format for Authority Data: [7]

100 1 $a Clemens, Samuel, $d 1835-1910

500 $w r $i alternate identity $a Twain, Mark, $d 1835-1910

Full reviews of MARC 21 changes are an important part of training plans. These changes are important from the practical perspective of learning how to encode data. They also reflect the key areas where RDA is different from AACR2.

RDA appendices D and E contain mappings between RDA elements and the MARC 21 authority and bibliographic formats. The appendices also suggest how to display data, demonstrating how RDA elements map to the International Standard Bibliographic Description (ISBD) and to existing conventions for AACR2 access points. The guidelines in the appendices show how to organize the data elements and add punctuation in a way that maintains continuity with existing display conventions.

RDA introduces a new way of thinking about cataloging and a new way of working with data elements. By using RDA, the cataloging community starts to record data that can support improved navigation and display. This does not immediately necessitate a new way to display data to the users. At the beginning, most of the data will be legacy data, so continuity in the presentation of data provides a consistent look. RDA data can be mapped to existing display conventions. As the balance between legacy data and RDA data shifts, and as new advances are made in the search and display of data, then RDA data can also be used in new presentations of data.

COORDINATED IMPLEMENTATION

The transition from AACR2 to RDA is not a process that individual catalogers or institutions face alone. The content of RDA was developed as an international initiative, with the formal participation of representatives from the four author countries: Australia, Canada, Great Britain, and the United States. Implementing RDA is also an international initiative, with coordination of plans and decisions among the four author countries. As early as 2007, the national libraries of the author countries, the National Library of Australia, Library and Archives Canada, the British Library, and the Library of Congress, announced their intention to coordinate implementation:

> To ensure a smooth transition to RDA, the four national libraries will work together where possible on implementation matters such as training, documentation and any national application decisions.[8]

In addition to the leadership role that each national library takes in its own country, implementation is further facilitated by cooperation between the countries.

Implementation will begin after a period of testing has been completed. The Library of Congress agreed to join with the National Library of Medicine and the National Library of Agriculture and carry out a formal testing of RDA before making a joint decision to implement RDA in the United States. The national libraries of Australia, Canada, and Great Britain will also test RDA, but these will be informal tests to prepare for national implementations and to inform implementation decisions.

The commitment to coordinated implementation was reaffirmed in 2009 in an e-mail to the RDA listserv, RDA-L (July 21, 2009). Marjorie Bloss, the RDA project manager, relayed a message from the members of the Committee of Principals who represent the four national libraries:

> The agreement among BL, LAC, LC, and NLA is still valid. The four national libraries have continued to work together and support the completion of the development of RDA. Since the issuance of the agreement, LC determined that it would—in collaboration with the U.S. National Agricultural Library and the National Library of Medicine—formally test RDA before it would implement RDA. On a parallel track, BL, LAC, and NLA would prepare for RDA implementation in their respective countries, working with their constituencies. The expectation is that, assuming the U.S. testing is positive, BL, LAC, and NLA will implement at about the same time in fall 2010.[9] In the event that LC decides not to implement at the conclusion of their test, implementation options will be reviewed by the four national libraries.[10]

The exchange of bibliographic data is a global activity. The American decision to carry out a formal test has delayed the implementation of RDA by a few months, but, if the U.S. testing is positive, the benefits of a coordinated implementation far outweigh the disadvantages of a short delay. In any case, the delay allows more time to prepare documentation and resources.

A key aspect of coordination is the alignment of decisions about which options and alternatives to follow. There are many places in RDA where there are alternative instructions or options to include or omit data (0.8). An example is the instruction for recording a statement of responsibility when the statement names more than one person (2.4.1.5). The main instruction does not include any instruction to omit names, regardless of the number of persons, etc. The instruction includes an optional omission:

2.4.1.5 *Optional Omission*

If a single statement of responsibility names more than three persons, families, or corporate bodies performing the same function, or with the same degree of responsibility, omit all but the first of each group of such persons, families, or bodies. Indicate the omission by summarizing what has been omitted in the language and script preferred by the agency preparing the description. Indicate that the summary was taken from a source outside the resource itself as instructed under 2.2.4.

The optional omission reflects a continuation of AACR2 practice. Thus, an institution could apply RDA using the optional omission, and retain greater consistency with past descriptive practice, or they could make the change, following the principle of representation consistently, simplifying transcription and supporting the capture and reuse of metadata from different environments.

It is possible for each agency to make its own decisions about alternatives and options. However, coordinated decisions improve the conditions for data exchange and present consistent data to the user. They also improve efficiency because one set of decisions are made collectively and maintained and updated for all. National application decisions ensure consistency within one country. If application decisions are coordinated at the international level, this will further improve the consistency of data, support the seamless exchange of records, as well as enable the shared use of the same training and procedure documents.

Related to national application decisions is the review of existing rule interpretations. The national libraries represented on the JSC had each developed and maintained interpretations of AACR2 rules. Some circumstances may still need to be addressed in the RDA environment, but many of these interpretations are no longer needed. The national libraries are reviewing their respective rule interpretations, eliminating many and rewriting some. These new guidelines are called policy statements instead of rule interpretations. The policy statements will be accessible through the Toolkit. For example, the Library of Congress reviewed its LC Rule Interpretations (LCRIs), eliminated many, and rewrote approximately one-quarter of them as LC Policy Statements (LCPSs).

Implementing RDA requires preparation and training. RDA introduces changes at both abstract and concrete levels. There are many topics that need to be covered during training. RDA has many points of similarity with its predecessor, AACR2, but the underlying framework is completely different because of the alignment with the FRBR and FRAD models. The transition to RDA requires developing some familiarity with the vocabulary and concepts that originate in the models. RDA includes scope for cataloger judgment; the cataloger needs to know the principles that are intended to guide judgments about the data that is important for the user. Many instructions in RDA reflect changes in practice, based on the alignment with FRBR and FRAD. There are changes in approach, such as the way RDA deals with content and carrier. There are changes in the wording of instructions. Some changes indicate a change in intent; some are simply changes to align with the vocabulary of FRBR and FRAD. RDA instructions are organized according to the FRBR and FRAD entities, thus AACR2 catalogers need some orientation for navigating through RDA. Using RDA also requires familiarity with MARC 21 changes. In addition, the standard is delivered as part of a Web tool. The Toolkit offers new features to improve and streamline work. Learning to navigate and use the Toolkit is another area of training. Some of these topics, such as learning the vocabulary of concepts of the FRBR and FRAD models, remain constant for all audiences. Depending on decisions about options, alternatives, and policies, training documentation could vary from one environment to another. Coordinated decisions about the options, alternatives, and policies means that training documentation can be shared easily across national boundaries, reducing the duplication of effort.

Coordinated implementation also permits the creation of procedure documents that can be widely used. The first two workflows, simple book and transcription, were documents prepared by the Library of Congress and approved by the Joint Steering Committee. Since they were written as general documents, options and alternatives were included, with a reminder that agency decisions were required. For example, from the simple book workflow: "*Optionally,* if your agency uses relationship designators from RDA Appendix I, record . . ." With coordinated implementation and the development of a uniform set of application decisions and policies, workflows could be streamlined and tightened. Each institution would not need to create in-house workflows documenting each decision but could simply start with workflows that incorporate the national libraries' application decisions.

The commitment to coordinated implementation facilitates the transition from AACR2 to RDA in concrete ways. It benefits the users of RDA data, with consistency across national boundaries, and it benefits the agencies and institutions that create the data by reducing duplication of efforts. Coordinated implementation permits a consistent application of RDA, and permits an efficient use and exchange of training and procedure documentation between countries.

NOTES

1. For the long term goals for RDA, see: Joint Steering Committee for Development of RDA, "Strategic Plan for RDA, 2005–2009" (5JSC/Strategic/1/Rev/2; November 1, 2007), www.rda-jsc.org/stratplan.html.
2. RDA Toolkit (Chicago: American Library Association; Ottawa: Canadian Library Association; London: Chartered Institute of Library and Information Professionals [CILIP], 2010–), www.rdatoolkit.org.
3. Joint Steering Committee for Development of RDA, "Constituency Review of Full Draft: Workflows: Book Workflow" (5JSC/RDA/Full draft/Workflows/Book; November 17, 2008), www.rda-jsc.org/docs/5rda-fulldraft-workflow-book.pdf; Joint Steering Committee for Development of RDA, "Constituency Review of Full Draft: Workflows: Transcription Workflow" (5JSC/RDA/Full draft/Workflows/Transcription; November 17, 2008), www.rda -jsc.org/docs/5rda-fulldraft-workflow-transcription.pdf.
4. More detail about changes to MARC 21 in the section "Encoding and Display of RDA Data," p. 83.
5. An overview of the changes was prepared by the Network Development and MARC Standards Office. Library of Congress Network Development and MARC Standards Office, "RDA in MARC (January 2010), www.loc.gov/marc/RDAinMARC29.html.

6. Extra spaces added in the example to improve legibility.

7. In the authority format, the control subfield w is also coded with the value "r" to indicate that there will be a relationship designation either in subfield i or subfield 4. Extra spaces added in the example to improve legibility.

8. "Coordinated implementation of RDA," Oct. 22, 2007, announcement archived at the JSC website as part of "Historic Documents, Archived RDA news," http://www.rda-jsc.org/rdaimpl.html.

9. Correction to the date of implementation: since the U.S. libraries estimate that they will require nine months to carry out and complete their formal testing, and testing begins after the first release of RDA, implementation is expected to take place in 2011.

10. Marjorie Bloss, "BL, LAC, LC, and NLA Implementation of RDA," e-mail to RDA-L, July 21, 2009, archived at http://www.mail-archive.com/rda-l@listserv.lac-bac.gc.ca/msg02860.html.

7

ADVANTAGES, PRESENT AND FUTURE

Changing to RDA brings some immediate improvements, but it also lays the groundwork for future improvements. There are advantages that will be seen on day one, advantages that will require a sufficiently large body of RDA data before they become apparent, advantages that necessitate software improvements to fully exploit the changes, and, finally, advantages that will be realized in future Web environments.

To achieve improvements, we need to start producing improved data now, data that is designed to support the user in their process of resource discovery, data that can be processed by humans and machines, data that is designed to function well in a range of environments, including the Web. Taking the analogy of a train, we need to switch railroad tracks because the current track is heading to a dead end. The current track has been very good, and has brought us this far, but it cannot take us through the next section. The track on which we began originated in the print-based world of the last century and does not extend well into the new networked online environment. We still want to head in the same general direction, to describe resources and give access to them, but we need to switch to a new track, so that we can keep moving forward.

Karen Coyle gives a summary of direction in which library data must move:

> Library data has been designed to be read and interpreted by librarians and users.
> . . . The emphasis is on the human user, even though the data today is stored in
> computer systems and displayed on a screen. The machine as user has not gotten
> a great deal of attention in the library cataloging environment.

> Now there's yet another potential user of library data, and that user is the Web and
> services that function on the Web. We know that our users go to the Web to do
> their research, to interact with other people, and to create their works. If we are
> to serve our users, then we need to deliver library services to users via the Web.
> But delivery over the network is not enough; our services must not only be *on* the
> Web, but need to be *of* the Web. The services cannot just pass through, but must
> live and interact on the Web. With Web-based data, we can use the vast informa-
> tion resources there to enhance our data by creating relationships between library
> data and information resources. This will not only increase opportunities for users

to discover the library and its resources, but will also increase the value of the data by allowing its use in a wide variety of contexts.[1]

RDA gives the library community the tool with which to start preparing for the next stage: library data on the Web. RDA is headed in the right direction, even if, as Coyle points out, it has not yet reached the point of being fully "of the Web."

> Both FRBR and RDA are realized as documents, which means that they are presented as human-readable concepts, not as computer code. In their document forms, neither can be acted on by computers, and neither can be moved seamlessly into the Web. . . . But the use of entities and relationships gives this whole that is FRBR + RDA some basic conceptual compatibility with the technology that is developing for the realization of the Semantic Web.[2]

The intention is to continue preparing RDA data to be "of the Web." This conceptual compatibility is an important step forward. It starts us down a new track, and this new track has long sight lines; there is a useful future for library data.

Four simple objectives guided the development of RDA:

0.4.2	Objectives
0.4.2.1	Responsiveness to user needs
0.4.2.2	Cost efficiency
0.4.2.3	Flexibility
0.4.2.4	Continuity

If one had to identify one overriding objective that defines RDA, responsiveness to user needs would be the one. But the flexibility objective is also very important because it is the objective that has prepared the groundwork for tomorrow:

> **0.4.2.3** *Flexibility*
> The data should function independently of the format, medium, or system used to store or communicate the data. They should be amenable to use in a variety of environments.

It is a simple objective, but achieving this objective is the key to making library data widely visible and usable, rather than having it locked into library catalogs and databases. RDA data can be encoded and stored as a MARC record, but it does not need to be encoded and stored in a MARC record. RDA data can be stored and used in databases of bibliographic and authority records, but RDA is not about creating records. RDA instructions are about data, and that data can be encoded, stored, and used in new ways. RDA data is not confined to the library catalog. It can be used in the current Web, and in the newly emerging semantic Web.

Bibliographic and authority data provides valuable pathways for users engaged in resource discovery. Libraries have a reputation for creating quality bibliographic and authority data, but it has been a struggle to make this data visible and usable in the Web environment. Implementing RDA will bring some changes that have an immediate impact, but it also puts into place the concepts and data design that will be required in the near future.

It is important to keep in mind that the advantages of using RDA are a mixture of immediate and future benefits. This chapter reviews the advantages of using RDA, looking at them from the perspective of users, institutions, and catalogers or metadata creators.

ADVANTAGES FOR USERS

Focus on the User

Like all resource description standards, the goal of RDA is to record and create data that helps the user. RDA has an advantage over past standards, such as AACR2, because it goes beyond a general sense of helping the user and actually maps between specific user tasks and different elements of bibliographic and authority data. In its alignment with the FRBR and FRAD conceptual models, RDA inherits and uses the valuable information from the models that shows how each attribute and relationship supports particular user tasks. The very first objective for RDA is responsiveness to user needs (0.4.2.1). This is not an abstract consideration, but is carried out into each section of RDA, realized with specific functional objectives written for each section, and incorporated at the specific level of the instructions. RDA instructions provide practical guidelines to record or create data that will support identified user tasks. Descriptions and access points are shaped neither by arbitrary case law nor by space-saving conventions such as the "rule of three." Focus on the user is translated into instructions that concretely serve the user, by recording data with the user's needs in mind. Thus the user should be better served by descriptions and access points that more accurately respond to their needs.

Data to Support Improved Navigation and Display

RDA is a content standard. It gives guidance about the data that should be recorded and instructs how to record it. It encourages the recording of sufficient data and parses the data into clearly identified data elements. RDA does not dictate how the data is displayed, nor how the search engine will use various elements to refine a search and drill down to the appropriate resource. RDA alone will not improve navigation and display because the data must be used appropriately by well-designed search engines and search interfaces. But the recording of clear, unambiguous data is a required step in the improvement of access to resources. The goal is to produce data that can support improved search and navigation, and improved displays of results.

Precisely Defined Data Elements

Many data elements in RDA correspond to information that was recorded in AACR2. However, AACR2 often had less granularity and precision when recording the data. Some information was embedded in long character strings as part of a nonspecific note or of another element. For example, AACR2 combined information about the type of tactile notation with the statement of extent: 320 leaves of computer braille. RDA has one specific element for extent and another for recording the type of tactile notation. The information is in clearly identified elements. In AACR2, different types of information were recorded in the same place. For example, in "other physical details," we can record a range of different information, depending on the class of materials that is being described: illustrative content, details about base material, projection speed, track configuration, etc. "Other physical details" is ambiguous. We cannot precisely identify the type of data that will be found there; it cannot be used as a precise way to search.

RDA segments the data into separate data elements. Different kinds of data are recorded in appropriate elements that are unambiguously defined and identified. Thus, it becomes possible to sort according to any of these data elements, to limit searches, to use the elements as a way to mine data or display data. At the time of first release and implementation, RDA data will still be encoded using MARC 21 data, and few changes have been made to take advantage of the full range of RDA data elements. But the definition of separate data elements positions RDA as a standard that can support improved navigation and display.

Data to Support Collocation

To build a display of results that conveys meaningful information to the user, it is important to group or cluster the results and show the degree of similarity or difference. It would be even better if we could label the clusters to identify the types of relationships between the resources in the set of results. If a user searches for *Robinson Crusoe* in a current catalog, the set of results is likely to be a mixture of resources: print and electronic editions of the original English text, motion pictures based on the original text, translations, audio books, criticisms, parodies, dramatizations. Often an edition of the original text does not even appear at the top of the list. The user has to read and decipher the results. A more useful display of results would group together all editions of the original English text, and then display other expressions, such as translations and spoken word versions of the text, then perhaps group together all the resources where "Robinson Crusoe" is the subject, followed by related works. The related works could be further grouped and identified according to the type of relationship, such as "based on," "parody of," and "dramatization of." Under the results for the original English text, results could be further grouped by carrier type, allowing the user to select quickly the appropriate resource.

RDA encourages the recording of sufficient data to support more precise collocation. Collocation requires the recording of relationships and the clear identification of those relationships. RDA emphasizes the importance of recording relationships and also encourages the recording of relationship designators. RDA includes three appendices of relationship designators: for relationships between a person, family, or corporate body and a resource, such as "author," "cartographer," or "photographer"; for relationships between works, expressions, manifestations and items, such as "based on" or "dramatization of"; and for relationships between persons, families, and corporate bodies, such as "alternate identity" or "member."

RDA also includes instructions that add precision to authorized access points, such as the instructions for constructing authorized access points representing expressions. Added precision in the access point also supports improved collocation.

RDA opens the door to new ways to improve collocation. RDA data is segmented into independent elements. Some of these elements are currently incorporated into access points, using a preset structure. The preset structure permits a certain amount of collocation that is precise but not flexible. However, when data is recorded as independent data elements, it can be stored, sorted, and presented in different ways. Each element has the potential to be used as a way to sort and collocate results. There is also the possibility of customizing the display of elements to respond to the needs of different user communities and to different types of queries.

Broadening the Horizon

RDA broadens the horizon in several ways. One area of change is the result of lessening the Anglo-American bias of AACR2 and aiming for greater internationalization. There are changes that aim to generalize the instructions and even out the treatment of different kinds of resources. For example, AACR2 rules about access points for sacred scriptures were much more detailed for the Bible than for other sacred scriptures. RDA aims for a consistent treatment of all sacred scriptures. Changes to make RDA adaptable for use in international contexts will be useful in terms of lessening potentially irritating practices, such as restrictions about the types of calendars and numbering that should be used.

For the user, broadening the horizon in the sense of breaking out of the library silo will have the most impact. There are two aspects to this broadening of the horizon: dialogue with other metadata communities and making RDA data available and usable outside the catalog.

Dialogue with Other Metadata Communities

During the development process, the Joint Steering Committee engaged in dialogue with other metadata communities. The JSC wanted to be aware of the metadata standards in related communities—such as archives, publishing, digital repositories—and to maintain alignment with these standards. One of the long term goals in the strategic plan is that RDA should be designed to "be usable primarily within the library community, but be capable of adaptation to meet the specific needs of other communities."[3] Thus, whether other communities choose to use RDA, or other communities work alongside the library producing similar data, alignment and compatibility of metadata reduces the disparities between similar data and enables the user to carry out comprehensive searches of data that may originate from different communities.

An example of alignment was the work on harmonizing RDA and ONIX terms for content and carrier types. ONIX is an international standard of the publishing industry. Representatives from two different communities met and together developed a common vocabulary. In this case, it was representatives of the developers of ONIX and representatives of the developers of RDA (the Joint Steering Committee and the RDA Editor). Both communities acknowledged the value of a shared vocabulary to improve the exchange of data. The "RDA/ONIX Framework for Resource Categorization" was the result of this dialogue, and it influenced the terminology used in the content, media, and carrier types used in RDA.[4]

RDA is a data content standard. It was deliberately written so that it would not be limited to the encoding standards and display conventions of the library environment. The standard will be used to describe library resources. It also presents an opportunity to break down barriers between different types of information resource repositories. RDA data could be encoded and displayed using standards and conventions used in other metadata communities.

RDA instructions apply to all types of resources; they apply to traditional library resources, such as print and electronic books and journals; they also apply to archival documents, documents in digital repositories, artifacts, etc. Many instructions were added, especially for archival resources, such as 2.10.6.7, Instruction for Recording the Date of Manufacture for Archival Resources.

RDA has flexibility, offers many options, and can be applied to all types of resources. RDA has the potential to be adopted by other metadata communities looking for a content standard. Even if RDA is used only in the library community, its alignment with other metadata standards and its instructions for well-formed metadata mean that users will experience greater consistency when searching data that originates from different communities.

Library Data Outside the Catalog

The catalog has been a silo. It has contained very useful data, but this data has been caught within a library-specific record structure and a library-specific database structure. As mentioned at the beginning of this chapter, getting data out of the library silo is an important next step. When RDA data is encoded in MARC records inside a library catalog, RDA data is not visible and usable except from within the catalog.

RDA data does not need to be stored in bibliographic and authority records. It is the way the library community will store and use this data at the beginning of implementation, and there are detailed mappings to show where RDA data should be encoded in MARC

21 bibliographic and authority records. But it is not the only way that a database can be structured. As part of the development process, RDA's editor produced a document called "RDA, FRBR/FRAD and Implementation Scenarios."[5] This document looks at using RDA in both current and future environments. The current scenarios are databases with bibliographic and authority records. The future scenario shows a database that mirrors the FRBR/FRAD model, where data is grouped not into traditional records but in records according to entity. The data about a particular resource is the data from all the records that are linked together. The links represent the relationships between the entities. This scenario is a first step in envisioning library data stored in a non-MARC database structure, and thus a first step in getting library data out of a library-specific database structure or silo.

RDA has the potential to be used as a metadata element set. The elements are already identified and defined in ways that are similar to the methods used for other metadata schema. To make an element set fully operable in the Web environment, the element set needs to be registered on the Web, along with any special vocabularies, and the terms or values that are used in those vocabularies. The DCMI/RDA Task Group[6] has been working to declare and register RDA element sets and vocabularies.[7] Thus the goal of getting RDA data visible and usable on the Web is more than just an idea. It is in the process of being realized.

Users do not commonly approach resource discovery thinking about the data silo in which they are likely to find relevant results. Relevant data might be in the library catalog, in the digital repository, in the museum's catalog, and in the finding aids of an archive. Alignment between metadata communities creates improved conditions for searching because data that has similar elements and structure can be searched together with the possibility of returning useful results even when the data originates from several communities. This becomes increasingly true as data comes out of silos and becomes visible and usable in a Web environment.

The user will benefit from the ways in which RDA aims to broaden horizons, maintain compatibility with other metadata communities, and prepare to use bibliographic and authority data in the Web environment. The objective of flexibility opened up the possibility of realizing these benefits. Implementing RDA means that the library community starts to prepare, so that these advantages can be realized.

Continuity

The objective of continuity lays the groundwork for implementing RDA today:

> **0.4.2.4** *Continuity*
>
> The data should be amenable to integration into existing databases (particularly those developed using AACR and related standards).

Continuity is important for the user because, at the moment of implementation, RDA will be used in existing databases and catalogs, encoded as MARC 21 bibliographic and authority records. Thus, even with all the focus on changes to make library data relevant and usable in the future, care was taken to ensure that RDA can be implemented and used in the existing environment.

As well, when RDA is first implemented, databases and catalogs will have a majority of records that were created using AACR. One of the positive effects of the ties between AACR2 and RDA is backward compatibility: data produced according to RDA can coexist in the same database or catalog with data produced according to earlier standards. Once there begins to be a sufficient quantity of RDA records, there will be scope for changes and improvements in the databases. But, during implementation, the goal is a near seamless crossover so that RDA records interfile with AACR2 records. For example, in order to achieve the objective of continuity, changes to access points were kept to a minimum. Any changes are ones that can be handled by global updates, such as the changes to access points for the Bible.

Thus, in the early days of implementation, the user will start seeing some improvements in the description of resources, with more precise details and more attention to relationships. But they will be able to search and use legacy data along with RDA data. Implementation will not bring a sudden change, but it will begin a gradual process of improvement.

Eliminating Confusing Description Practices

AACR was originally used in the card catalog environment. Some description practices were not particularly helpful for the user, but were dictated by the shortage of space on a 3 x 5 catalog card. Thus, AACR2 had many rules where the cataloger was instructed to use an abbreviation instead of the full word. This occurred in places where the cataloger transcribed or simply recorded data. RDA does not introduce abbreviations into the description. In an element that is transcribed, such as the edition statement, the cataloger transcribes exactly, and if the source of information has an abbreviation, then the cataloger transcribes the abbreviation. But the cataloger does not introduce an abbreviation when the source of information shows the complete word. In RDA, the principle of representation is important. When transcribing, the cataloger is instructed to take what they see, and thus the description matches how the resource presents itself. The user will have no doubts because there is a close correspondence between the resource and the description.

In following the principle of transcription, RDA also lessens the number of instances where there are exceptions to transcription, such as the AACR2 rule to omit data if there are three or more persons or corporate bodies performing the same function. The main instruction in RDA directs the cataloger to record them all. There is an optional omission, but the main instruction is to transcribe what we see. The RDA description will match the resource's representation of itself. It also means that all the names are visible and usable for finding and identifying the resource. If the optional omission is used, the cataloger inserts a summary phrase, such as [and six others], instead of the ambiguous abbreviation [et al.].

In an element where data is recorded instead of transcribed, such as extent, the cataloger uses the full word, such as pages or volumes. Full words are not ambiguous. Abbreviations can be misinterpreted, and are also difficult to use in searches. Similarly, RDA eliminates Latin abbreviations and replaces them with an explanatory phrase.

RDA has a flexible and extensible framework for the content and technical description of all types of resources. The framework, based on the entities, attributes, and relationships identified in the FRBR and FRAD models, provides a way to describe known resources and resources that have yet to be developed. The framework shapes and defines the RDA element set. It enables the cataloger to capture the relevant data about a new resource and proceed to complete the description. The user benefits because there are no delays. RDA's framework also includes a way to categorize content, media, and carrier information by using a grid or framework of three elements: content, media, and carrier types. This grid can also be applied to the description of known and new types of resources. The grid requires the presence of data in all the elements, but these elements do not need to be displayed as a list of terms. Combinations of the terms can then be mapped to show meaningful phrases or icons to the user. The data is recorded, and it can then be presented to the user in different ways. The advantage to the user will be influenced by how well the data is used both in resource discovery and in data display.

RDA's instructions for description are intended to record clear, unambiguous data and to match the resource's representation of itself as closely as possible. Descriptive practices that served as shortcuts in the card catalog environment are eliminated because they do not serve the user well.

ADVANTAGES FOR INSTITUTIONS

All the advantages for the user are also advantages for libraries and similar institutions. Most institutions have as their first goal to serve their users. Thus, changes that support an improved resource discovery experience for the user are improvements that allow the institution to better serve their user population. In addition, the staff of the institution use bibliographic and authority data to carry out responsibilities such as responding to information requests, developing the collection, or acquiring resources. As a group of users, the institution's staff also benefit from data that is more precisely defined and that supports better navigation and display.

Institutions are often concerned with their visibility, both in terms of making their institution known and of reminding their user population of the resources available through the institution. Moving toward the goal of making library data usable in Web environments benefits the institutions because it brings visibility to the institutions' collections and increases the institution's Web presence.

Depending on the identity and mission of an institution, the changes that make RDA adaptable for use in an international context will have varying importance. There was a conscious effort to remove the Anglo-American bias, with adjustments to instructions about language, script, numbering, and calendars. The degree of change is not great, but it signals that RDA is designed so that it can be adapted for use in a range of languages and cultures. RDA instructions are organized so that most of them are general and apply to all resources, with some specific instructions and exceptions following the general ones. This generalization of instructions also evens out the treatment of resources, such as sacred scriptures, because the same general instructions apply to all. RDA's move away from the Anglo-American bias brings advantages at the practical level of applying the instructions in different contexts, and of producing descriptions that make sense to different user populations. It makes RDA a more equitable standard.

The defining characteristic of RDA is its alignment with the FRBR and FRAD conceptual models, and its consistency with the International Cataloguing Principles. RDA uses the concepts, vocabulary, and principles that are recognized and used by the international cataloging community. In the networked online world, libraries operate in a global environment. For example, alignment with the FRBR and FRAD models means that the RDA community will be able to take advantage of international innovations that are based on the same conceptual framework. The ability of institutions to take advantage of this global environment, to work together and to use and exchange data rests on the assumption of sufficient similarities in approach.

RDA is released as part of RDA Toolkit, a Web tool. The Toolkit includes features that facilitate the use of RDA. There are different ways to view and use the content of the standard. RDA instructions can be accessed through the table of contents, through searches, and through tools such as the Element Set View or workflows. The Toolkit accommodates different styles of learning and working. It includes workflows and mappings that permit staff to move quickly into producing resource descriptions and access points according to the new standard. Workflows and mappings can also be customized to incorporate the institution's preferences and local procedures. The institution can roll their previous training and local procedure documents into a set of workflows and mappings, thereby keeping all documentation in one place and linked to the latest version of the standard. Workflows and mappings can also be shared with the cataloging community, and support a consistent application of RDA. The Toolkit offers ways to increase efficiency in the workplace.

Changing to RDA also sets the stage to realize advantages in efficiency. Close adherence to the principle of representation simplifies the process of transcription and also aligns the resource's representation of itself with the description, reinforcing the user's identification of the resource. It also permits the reuse of metadata. RDA actually addresses the automated capture and reuse of metadata (the alternative at 1.7.1), and it is also included as part of the section on RDA's key features:

0.1   *Key Features*

. . .

RDA is designed to take advantage of the efficiencies and flexibility in data capture, storage, retrieval, and display made possible with new database technologies, but to be compatible as well with the legacy technologies still used in many resource discovery applications

Designing RDA to take advantage of future scenarios for the capture, storage, retrieval, and display of data is an important advantage because it positions RDA data to operate effectively in the Web environment, both current and emerging. It also sets the stage to take advantage of the efficiencies that can be realized with new technologies, such as streamlined workflows with automated data capture and reuse, as well as improved database structures that mirror the FRBR and FRAD models and replace duplicated data with links. Relevancy and return on investment are important for institutions that assign staff and financial resources to the task of resource description.

RDA 0.1 also mentions continuity. Continuity is as important for institutions as it is for users. RDA was designed to enable a smooth transition, by balancing the need for flexibility for the future with the need for continuity with the past.

ADVANTAGES FOR CATALOGERS AND METADATA CREATORS

All the advantages for users and for institutions are also advantages for the cataloger or metadata creator. The cataloger aims to serve the needs of the user. RDA gives the cataloger concrete guidance to respond to the user's needs and to record data that matches the specific user tasks. Most catalogers work as part of an institution. When the use of RDA supports the institution's goals, the use of RDA enables the cataloger to achieve the institution's goals.

RDA also has advantages that will be most evident for the cataloger. RDA is a detailed set of instructions, but it also leaves place for cataloger judgment. RDA is built on the theoretical framework expressed in the FRBR and FRAD models, and its design is guided by principles. RDA provides a theoretical structure to guide the cataloger in making judgments. It provides a fundamental orientation and specific functional objectives; then, in some instructions, it leaves room for the cataloger to judge "if considered important." In these cases, the cataloger applies the theory and functional objectives to decide whether the data will assist the user in completing a task such as finding or identifying, etc.

Positioning library data so that it has a role in the future is important for users and institutions. It has great importance for catalogers who devote their time and energy to producing quality bibliographic and authority data. The data we create has a future. It will not disappear if the MARC environment comes to an end. RDA provides a new way of envisioning bibliographic and authority data that is not tied to a particular encoding system, record structure, or display. RDA's instructions lead to the production of data that can continue to be relevant in new database environments and can be used effectively in the wider environment of the Web.

RDA makes the cataloger's work relevant for the twenty-first century, but it is also designed so that it can be implemented in the existing environment. RDA represents a major change in approach, but leaves open the door for a gradual transition. Many instructions are unchanged in intention, even though the words and the location of the instruction have changed. Several instructions represent a change in practice from AACR2, but also include options to follow an alternative that is closer to previous practice. RDA builds on the strengths of AACR2. At the same time, it also brings a much more consistent and logical approach to the process of resource description.

There are many changes that will make cataloging easier. For example, there are fewer exceptions when transcribing data. Another example is the more logical and consistent categorization of content and carrier that replaces the general material designations. No longer will a cataloger need to stop and wait for guidance about which GMD to use when describing a new type of resource. The cataloger completes the description, recording data in the elements for content, media and carrier types, and moves on. Mappings for display to the user can always be adjusted and changed later. The data stays the same.

RDA has a consistent approach for the description of all types of resources. Wherever possible, RDA generalized instructions to apply to all resources and reduced exceptions. If the general instruction is not sufficient, then specific instructions for special types of resources follow. For example, instructions for serials and integrating resources are not segregated into a separate section, but integrated, with special instructions only added as required. This approach also makes it easier to apply the instructions to new types of resources.

RDA is part of the Web tool RDA Toolkit. The Toolkit offers several ways to use the standard and to integrate it efficiently into daily work. There are different views of the content and different ways to search and organize the instructions. There are practical documents, such as the workflows and mappings, that allow cataloging staff to zero in on particular tasks. The flexibility of the Toolkit means that it can match different learning styles, making it easier to learn and easier to teach. The customization feature for workflows and mappings is a way to integrate local policies and procedures into customized documents that are stored in the Toolkit. Customized documents with local documentation are found in the same place as the standard; they also link to the latest version of the standard, making them less likely to become quickly outdated. The Toolkit promotes the following of standards by providing several ways to use RDA efficiently within the daily work environment.

Not all advantages will be immediately apparent on the first day of implementation. Implementation should be seen as a process that begins with the transition from AACR2 to RDA, fitting within the parameters of the current environment. But there will be changes from day one, and catalogers will be the first ones to benefit because they will start using the new logical and consistent standard, built on principles and theory and aimed at improving resource discovery for the user. As the catalogers build the body of RDA data, users will start to see the benefits of a standard that puts their needs at the center.

NOTES

1. Karen Coyle, "RDA Vocabularies for a Twenty-First-Century Data Environment." *Library Technology Reports* 46, no 2 (2010), p. 6.

2. Ibid., p. 9.

3. Joint Steering Committee for Development of RDA, "Strategic Plan for RDA, 2005–2009" (5JSC/Strategic/1/Rev/2; November 1, 2007), www.rda-jsc.org/stratplan.html (last updated: July 1, 2009).

4. "RDA/ONIX Framework for Resource Categorization" (5JSC/Chair/10; August 3, 2006), www.rda-jsc.org/docs/5chair10.pdf.

5. Tom Delsey, "RDA, FRBR/FRAD and Implementation Scenarios" (5JSC/Editor/4; 2008), www.rda-jsc.org/docs/5editor4.pdf.

6. DCMI = Dublin Core Metadata initiative. The DCMI/RDA Task Group wiki: http://dublincore .org/dcmirdataskgroup/.

7. The RDA (Resource Description and Access) Vocabularies at the National Science Digital Library Metadata Registry (NSDL): http://metadataregistry.org/rdabrowse.htm.

SELECTED RESOURCES AND READINGS

RDA

RDA Toolkit. Chicago: American Library Association; Ottawa: Canadian Library Association; London: Chartered Institute of Library and Information Professionals (CILIP), 2010– . www.rdatoolkit.org.

Resource Description and Access. Chicago: American Library Association; Ottawa: Canadian Library Association; London: Chartered Institute of Library and Information Professionals (CILIP), 2010– . In RDA Toolkit, www.rdatoolkit.org.

RESOURCES FOR TRAINING AND IMPLEMENTATION

Documents from the JSC and the MARC Standards Office

Delsey, Tom. "RDA Database Implementation Scenarios." 5JSC/Editor/2; January 14, 2007. www.rda-jsc.org/docs/5editor2.pdf.

_____. "RDA, FRBR/FRAD and Implementation Scenarios." 5JSC/Editor/4; 2008. www.rda-jsc.org/docs/5editor4.pdf.

Joint Steering Committee for Development of RDA. "Changes to AACR2 Instructions." 5JSC/Sec/7/Rev; July 2, 2009. www.rda-jsc.org/docs/5sec7rev.pdf.

_____. "Constituency Review of Full Draft: Workflows: Book Workflow." 5JSC/RDA/Full draft/Workflows/Book; November 17, 2008. www.rda-jsc.org/docs/5rda-fulldraft-workflow-book.pdf.

_____. "Constituency Review of Full Draft: Workflows: Transcription Workflow." 5JSC/RDA/Full draft/Workflows/Transcription; November 17, 2008. www.rda-jsc.org/docs/5rda-fulldraft-workflow-transcription.pdf.

_____. "Issues Deferred until after the First Release of RDA." 5JSC/RDA/Sec/6; November 6, 2008. www.rda-jsc.org/docs/5sec6.pdf.

Library of Congress Network Development nd MARC Standards Office. "RDA in MARC." January 2010. www.loc.gov/marc/RDAinMARC29.html.

Presentations

Many of the presentations listed at the Joint Steering Committee website, www.rda-jsc.org/rdapresentations.html, include links to the content of the presentations. This list is constantly updated.

Webcasts

The following can be used as instructional modules.

Tillett, Barbara. "Resource Description and Access: Background/Overview." May 14, 2008. www.loc.gov/today/cyberlc/feature_wdesc.php?rec=4320.

_____. "Cataloging Principles and RDA." June 10, 2008. www.loc.gov/today/cyberlc/feature_wdesc.php?rec=4327.

_____. "FRBR: Things You Should Know, but Were Afraid to Ask." March 4, 2009. www.loc.gov/today/cyberlc/feature_wdesc.php?rec=4554.

_____. "RDA Changes from AACR2 for Texts." January 12, 2010. www.loc.gov/today/cyberlc/feature_wdesc.php?rec=4863.

_____. "RDA: Antecedents y aspectos de su implementacion." August 13, 2009. www.loc.gov/today/cyberlc/feature_wdesc.php?rec=4736.

Documents from the Joint Steering Committee Website

All the documents on the Joint Steering Committee for Development of RDA website (www.rda-jsc.org/rda.html) are of interest and use. Attention is drawn to the following documents as an introduction to RDA.

Joint Steering Committee for Development of RDA. "RDA Element Analysis." 5JSC/RDA/Element analysis/Rev/2; October 26, 2008. www.rda-jsc .org/docs/5rda-elementanalysisrev2.pdf.

_____. "RDA FAQ." www.rda-jsc.org/rdafaq.html.

_____. "RDA—Resource Description and Access: A Prospectus." 5JSC/RDA/Prospectus/Rev/7; July 1, 2009). www.rda-jsc.org/rdaprospectus.html.

_____. *RDA*, "Resource Description and Access: Objectives and Principles." JSC/RDA/Objectives and Principles/Rev/3; July 1, 2009. www.rda-jsc .org/docs/5rda-objectivesrev3.pdf.

_____. "RDA Core Elements and FRBR User Tasks." 5JSC/Chair/15; November 5, 2008. www.rda-jsc .org/docs/5chair15.pdf.

_____. "Strategic Plan for RDA, 2005–2009." 5JSC/ Strategic/1/Rev/2; November 1, 2007. www.rda-jsc .org/stratplan.html. Last updated: July 1, 2009.

_____. "RDA Scope and Structure." JSC/RDA/ Scope/Rev/4; July 1, 2009. www.rda-jsc.org/docs/ 5rda-scoperev4.pdf.

_____. "Using RDA with Bibliographic and Authority Records." 5JSC/Chair/14; November 3, 2008. www .rda-jsc.org/docs/5chair14.pdf.

RDA AND OTHER METADATA COMMUNITIES

Beacom, Matthew. "Cataloging Cultural Objects (CCO), Resource Description and Access (RDA), and the Future of Metadata Content." *VRA Bulletin* 34, no. 1 (2007): 81–85.

Bowen, Jennifer. "Metadata to Support Next-Generation Library Resource Discovery: Lessons from the Extensible Catalog, Phase 1." *Information Technology & Libraries* 27, no. 2 (2008): 5–19.

Coyle, Karen. "RDA Vocabularies for a Twenty-First-Century Data Environment." *Library Technology Reports* 46, no 2 (2010): 5–38 (series of 4 articles in issue no. 2).

DCMI/RDA Task Group Wiki. Dublin Core Metadata Initiative website: http://dublincore.org/dcmirda taskgroup/.

Dunsire, Gordon. "Distinguishing Content from Carrier: The RDA/Onix Framework for Resource Categorization." *D-Lib Magazine* 13, no. 1/2 (2007). www.dlib.org/dlib/january07/dunsire/01dunsire .html.

Hillman, Diane, Karen Coyle, Jon Phipps, and Gordon Dunsire. "RDA Vocabularies: Process, Outcome, Use." *D-Lib Magazine* 16, no. 1/2 (2010). www.dlib .org/dlib/january10/hillmann/01hillmann.html

"RDA/ONIX Initiative Update." September 27, 2006. www.rda-jsc.org/rdaonixann.html.

FRBR FAMILY OF CONCEPTUAL MODELS: FRBR, FRAD, FRSAD

For an extensive list of publications about FRBR, see the FRBR Review Group's "FRBR Bibliography," www.ifla.org/en/node/881. A similar bibliography for publications about FRAD is currently being developed.

Bowen, Jennifer. "FRBR: Coming Soon to Your Library?" *Library Resources & Technical Services* 49, no. 3 (2005): 175–188.

Carlyle, Allyson. "Understanding FRBR as a Conceptual Model: FRBR and the Bibliographic Universe." *Library Resources & Technical Services* 50, no. 4 (2006): 264–273.

Dickey, Timothy J. "FRBRization of a Library Catalog: Better Collocation of Records, Leading to Enhanced Search, Retrieval, and Display." *Information Technology & Libraries* 27, no. 1 (2008): 23–32.

IFLA Study Group on the Functional Requirements for Bibliographic Records. *Functional Requirements for Bibliographic Records: Final Report.* Munich: Saur, 1998. Also online: www.ifla.org/en/publications/ functional-requirements-for-bibliographic -records.

IFLA Working Group on Functional Requirements and Numbering of Authority Records (FRANAR). *Functional Requirements for Authority Data: A Conceptual Model.* Munich: Saur, 2009.

IFLA Working Group on Functional Requirements of Subject Authority Records (FRASAR). *Functional Requirements for Subject Authority Data,* 2nd draft. June 10, 2009. www.ifla.org/en/node/1297.

Le Boeuf, Patrick, ed. *Functional Requirements for Bibliographic Records (FRBR): Hype or Cure-All?*

Binghampton, NY: Haworth, 2005. Published simultaneously as vol. 39, no. 3/4 of *Cataloging & Classification Quarterly.*

Madison, Olivia M. A. "The Origins of the IFLA Study on Functional Requirements for Bibliographic Records." *Cataloging & Classification Quarterly* 39, no. 3/4 (2005): 15–37.

_____. "Utilizing the FRBR Framework in Designing User-Focused Digital Content and Access Systems." *Library Resources & Technical Services* 50, no. 1 (2006): 10–15.

Maxwell, Robert L. *FRBR: A Guide for the Perplexed.* Chicago: American Library Association, 2008.

O'Neill, Edward T. "FRBR: Functional Requirements for Bibliographic Records: Application of the Entity-Relationship Model to 'Humphry Clinker.'" *Library Resources & Technical Services* 46, no. 4 (2002): 150–159.

Oliver, Chris. "FRBR Is Everywhere, but What Happened to the Format Variation Issue? Content Versus Carrier in FRBR." *Serials Librarian* 45, no. 4 (2004): 27–36.

Patton, Glenn E. "From FRBR to FRAD: Extending the Model." Paper given at the 2009 IFLA Annual Conference in Milan, Italy, Division IV, Bibliographic Control, session 215. www.ifla.org/files/hq/papersifla75/215-patton-en.pdf.

Riva, Pat. "Introducing the Functional Requirements for Bibliographic Records and Related IFLA Developments." *Bulletin of the American Society for Information Science & Technology* 33, no. 6 (2007): 7–11. www.asis.org/Bulletin/Aug-07/Riva.pdf.

Taylor, Arlene G. *Understanding FRBR: What It Is and How It Will Affect Our Retrieval Tools.* Westport, CT: Libraries Unlimited, 2007.

Tillett, Barbara. "FRBR and Cataloging for the Future." *Cataloging & Classification Quarterly* 39, no. 3/4 (2005): 197–205.

_____. *What Is FRBR? A Conceptual Model for the Bibliographic Universe.* Washington, DC: Cataloging Distribution Service, Library of Congress, 2004. www.loc.gov/cds/downloads/FRBR.PDF.

Yee, Martha M. "FRBRrization: A Method for Turning Online Public Finding Lists into Online Public Catalogs." *Information Technology & Libraries* 24, no. 2 (2005): 77–95.

Zeng, Marcia Lee, and Maya Žumer. "Introducing FRSAD and Mapping It with SKOS and Other Models. Paper given at the 2009 IFLA Conference in Milan, Italy, Classification and Indexing Section, session 200. www.ifla.org/files/hq/papers/ifla75/200-zeng-en.pdf.

GENERAL ARTICLES ABOUT RDA

This list excludes articles that refer frequently to aspects of RDA that are now obsolete or that describe/debate a single aspect.

Adamich, Tom. "RDA and School Libraries: Where Are We Going and Why Can't We Keep AACR2?" *Technicalities* 29, no. 6 (2009): 12–15.

Chapman, Ann. "RDA: A Cataloguing Code for the 21st Century." *Library & Information Update* 7, no. 9 (2008): 28–30.

Curran, Mary. "Serials in RDA: A Starter's Tour and Kit." *Serials Librarian* 57, no. 4 (2009): 306–324.

Hitchens, Alison, and Ellen Symons. "Preparing Catalogers for RDA Training." *Cataloging & Classification Quarterly* 47, no. 8 (2009): 691–707.

Knight, F. Tim. "Cataloguing Rules: the Road to RDA." *TALL Quarterly* 28, no. 2/3 (2009). http://hdl.handle.net/ 10315/2550.

Miksa, Shawne D. "Resource Description and Access (RDA) and New Research Potentials." *Bulletin of the American Society for Information Science & Technology* 35, no. 5 (2009): 47–51.

Moore, Julie Renee. "RDA: New Cataloging Rules, Coming Soon to a Library near You!" *Library Hi Tech News* 23, no. 9 (2006): 12–16.

Oliver, Chris. "Changing to RDA." Feliciter 53, no. 5 (2007): 250–253. Also online: www.rda-jsc.org/docs/felicitervol53no7p250-253.pdf.

Parent, Ingrid. "Les RDA pour un monde numérique." Argus 38, no. 1 (2009): 27–29.

Riva, Pat, and Natalie Bellemare. "La norme RDA: Outil mondial et intégration locale. " Argus 38, no. 1 (2009): 23–26.

DEVELOPMENT OF RDA

ALCTS CC:DA Task Force on Consistency across Part 1 of AACR. "Documents." www.libraries.psu .edu/tas/jca/ccda/tf-con1.html.

ALCTS CC:DA Task Force on Rule 0.24. "Overview and Recommendations Concerning Revision of Rule 0.24." 4JSC/ALA/30; August 16, 1999. www .libraries.psu.edu/tas/jca/ccda/docs/tf-024h.pdf

Delsey, Tom. "Categorization of Content and Carrier." 5JSC/RDA/Part A/Categorization; August 4, 2006. www.rda-jsc.org/docs/5rda-parta-categorization .pdf.

_____. "Functional Analysis of the MARC 21 Bibliographic and Holdings Formats, 2nd Revision." Prepared for the Network Development and MARC Standards Office, Library of Congress, 2003, updated by NDMSO 2006. www.loc.gov/ marc/marc-functional-analysis/functional -analysis.html.

_____. "The Logical Structure of the Anglo-American Cataloguing Rules." 1998. www.rda-jsc.org/docs .html#logical.

Howarth, Lynne C., and Jean Weihs. "Making the Link: AACR to RDA: Part 1: Setting the Stage." *Cataloging & Classification Quarterly* 45, no. 2 (2007): 3–18. See also the other three articles in this series:

> Howarth, Lynne C., and Jean Weihs. "Enigma Variations: Parsing the Riddle of Main Entry and The 'Rule of Three' from AACR2 to RDA." *Cataloging & Classification Quarterly* 46, no. 2 (2008): 201–220.

> Weihs, Jean, and Lynne C. Howarth. "Designating Materials: From 'Germane Terms' to Element Types." *Cataloging & Classification Quarterly* 45, no. 4 (2008): 3–24.

> _____. "Uniform Titles from AACR to RDA." *Cataloging & Classification Quarterly* 46, no. 4 (2008): 362–384.

IFLA Meetings of Experts on an International Cataloguing Code (IME-ICC). "Statement of International Cataloguing Principles." 2009. www.ifla .org/files/cataloguing/icp/icp_2009-en.pdf.

Tillett, Barbara. "International Cataloguing Principles (ICP) Report." Paper given at the 2009 IFLA Conference in Milan, Italy, Division IV, Bibliographic Control, session 215. www.ifla.org/ files/hq/papers/ifla75/215-tillett-en.pdf.

International Conference on the Principles and Future Development of AACR

Toronto, Ontario, Canada, October 23–25, 1997. www.rda-jsc.org/intlconf1.html.

Conference Papers (versions posted prior to the conference)

Delsey, Tom. "Modeling the Logic of AACR." http://epe.lac-bac.gc.ca/100/200/300/jsc_aacr/ modeling/r-bibun.pdf.

Fattahi, Rahmatollah. "AACR2 and Catalogue Production Technology: The Relevance of Cataloguing Principles to the Online Environment." http://epe.lac-bac.c.ca/100/200/ 300/jsc_aacr/aacr_cat/ r-aacr2.pdf.

Gorman, Michael and Pat Oddy. "The Anglo-American Cataloguing Rules, Second Edition: Their History and Principles." http://epe.lac-bac .gc.ca/100/200/ 300/jsc_aacr/aacr_sec/r-aacr2e.pdf.

Hagler, Ronald. "Access Points for Works." http://epe.lac-bac.gc.ca/100/200/300/jsc_aacr/ access/r-access.pdf.

Howarth, Lynne C. "Content versus Carrier." http://epe.lac-bac.gc.ca/100/200/300/jsc_aacr/ content/rcarrier.pdf.

Hyrons, Jean and Crystal Graham. "Issues Related to Seriality." http://epe.lac-bac.gc.ca/100/200/300/ jsc_aacr/issues/r-serial.pdf.

Ridley, Mick. "Beyond MARC." http://epe.lac-bac .gc.ca/100/200/300/jsc_aacr/beyond/r-beyond.htm.

Vellucci, Sherry L. "Bibliographic Relationships." http://epe.lac-bac.gc.ca/100/200/300/jsc_aacr/ bib_rel/r-bibrel.pdf.

Yee, Martha M. "What is a Work?" http://epe.lac-bac .gc.ca/100/200/300/jsc_aacr/whatis/r-whatis.pdf.

Published Proceedings

Weihs, Jean, ed. *The Principles and Future of AACR: Proceedings of the International Conference on the Principles and Future Development of AACR.* Toronto, Ontario, Canada, October 23–27, 1997.

Ottawa: Canadian Library Association; London: Library Association Publishing; Chicago: American Library Association, 1998.

Action Items

Joint Steering Committee for Development of RDA. International Conference on the Future Development of AACR. "Action Items, Progress Report, July 2005." www.rda-jsc.org/intlconf2 .html.

Joint Steering Committee for Development of RDA. Historic documents. www.rda-jsc.org/docs.html.

MARC Proposals (www.loc.gov/marc/marbi/list-p.html)

No. 2008-05/1: "Encoding RDA: Introduction and Principles." www.loc.gov/marc/marbi/2008/ 2008-05-1.html.

No. 2008-05/4: "Enhancing Field 502 (Dissertation Note) of the MARC 21 Bibliographic Format." www.loc.gov/marc/marbi/2008/2008-05-4.html.

No. 2009-01/1: "New Data Elements in the MARC21 Authority Format." www.loc.gov/marc/marbi/ 2009/2009-01-1.html.

No. 2009-01/2: "New Content Designation for RDA Element: Content Type, Media Type, Carrier Type." www.loc.gov/marc/marbi/2009/2009-01-2 .html.

No. 2009-01/3: "Identifying Work, Expression, and Manifestation Records in the MARC 21 Bibliographic and Authority Formats." www.loc.gov/marc/marbi/ 2009/2009-01-3.html.

No. 2009-06/1: "Accommodating Relationship Designators for RDA Appendix J and K in MARC 21 Bibliographic and Authority Formats." www.loc.gov/marc/marbi/2009/2009-06-1.html.

No. 2009-06/2: "Transcribing Series and Subseries ISSNs." www.loc.gov/marc/marbi/ 2009/ 2009-06-2.html.

No. 2009-06/3: "New Coded Values for RDA Media Carriers in the MARC 21 Bibliographic Format." www.loc.gov/marc/marbi/2009/2009-06-3.html.

No. 2010-03: "Recording Place and Date of Capture in the MARC21 Bibliographic Format." www.loc.gov/marc/marbi/ 2010/2010-03.html.

No. 2010-04: "New Data Elements in the MARC 21 Authority and Bibliographic Format for Works and Expressions." www.loc.gov/marc/marbi/ 2010/2010-04.html.

INDEX

governance structure for AACR2/
　　RDA, 37–38
granularity, 59, 94
grid of three elements, 50, 53, 70–71,
　　99

H

headings (AACR2 term) as access
　　points, 33
human processing of data, 42, 51,
　　59, 92

I

identifier (FRAD entity), 23
identifiers, recording of, 10
"identify" as user task
　　authority data, 16
　　bibliographic data, 15
IFLA (International Federation of
　　Library Associations)
　　and FRBR study group, 8, 14
　　ISBD standard, 6
　　Statement of International
　　　Cataloguing Principles, 8
　　Working Group on Functional
　　　Requirements and Numbering
　　　of Authority Records
　　　(FRANAR), 14
implementation by national
　　libraries, coordination of, 73,
　　86–89, 90n9
inaccuracies, transcription of, 63
inherent attributes, 20
inherent relationships, 35n8
institutions, benefits of RDA for,
　　99–101
integrated library systems and
　　cataloging services, 82
integrating resources
　　inaccuracies in, 63
　　as mode of issuance, 56
International Cataloguing Principles
　　(ICP) (Paris Principles)
　　alignment of RDA with, 12, 47,
　　　64, 100
　　history, 6, 9
　　influence on AACR, 38
International Conference on Cata-
　　loguing Principles (1961), 6
　　See also International Cataloguing
　　　Principles (ICP) (Paris
　　　Principles)

International Conference on
　　the Principles & Future
　　Development of AACR
　　(Toronto, 1997), 10–11, 44
international resource description
　　standards, 6
international scope of RDA, 4, 6–12
International Standard
　　Bibliographic Description. *See*
　　ISBD (International Standard
　　Bibliographic Description)
internationalization
　　of AACR2, 38–39
　　and benefits to institutions, 100
　　"preferred by the agency creating
　　　the data," 11
　　and reduction of Anglo-
　　　American bias in RDA, 95, 100
interoperability as Paris principle, 6
ISBD (International Standard
　　Bibliographic Description)
　　contrast to RDA presentation, 2,
　　　5n4
　　mappings to RDA data, 86
　　as possible structure for
　　　reorganizing AACR2, 43
　　as standard, 6, 7
ISBN (International Standard Book
　　Number), 10
ISO (International Organization for
　　Standardization), 9
ISSN (International Standard Serial
　　Number), 10
items (entity)
　　as exemplars of manifestations,
　　　21
　　as FRBR Group 1 entity, 18

J

Johnson, Bruce, 43
joint authorship. *See* creators
Joint Steering Committee. *See* JSC
　　(Joint Steering Committee)
Joint Steering Committee for
　　Revision of AACR
　　decision to revise AACR2 in
　　　2004, 44–45
　　history, 42–43
　　international commenting
　　　process for RDA, 11–12
　　International Conference on
　　　the Principles & Future

Development of AACR
　　(Toronto, 1997), 10–11
Joint Steering Committee for the
　　Development of RDA, 45n1
JSC (Joint Steering Committee)
　　dialogue with other metadata
　　　communities, 95–96
　　governance structure, 37–38, 39
　　and vocabulary for content,
　　　media, and carrier types, 51
"justify" as user task, 16

L

languages and scripts, multiple
　　Anglo-American bias in AACR2,
　　　100
　　data mapped to another
　　　language, 72n6
　　example in authorized access
　　　point, 69
　　instructions for, 11
　　usability of RDA for, 4
learning preferences, 82–83, 100
legacy data from AACR2,
　　compatibility with, 4, 83, 86,
　　97–98
levels of description, absence of, 61
Library and Archives Canada, 86
library and information workers
　　and user tasks, 15, 16–17
　　See also catalogers
library catalogs, 4–5
　　See also displays
library data outside the catalog, 96–97
Library of Congress, 38, 86, 87
Library of Congress Rule
　　Interpretations, 88
limiting a search
　　in RDA Toolkit, 76
　　and use of content, media, and
　　　carrier types, 55
local policies and procedures, 79,
　　89, 100
long titles, transcription of, 63–64

M

machine processing of data
　　ability for, 71, 84, 91
　　difficulty with in AACR2, 58
　　and sharing of records, 41
　　See also data capture; global
　　　changes and compatibility

You may also be interested in

RDA Toolkit: Use the resources in the online RDA Toolkit to navigate from AACR2 to RDA. RDA—included in the toolkit—is the new unified standard for resource description and access, designed for the digital world and an expanding universe of metadata users. The RDA Toolkit also includes user-created and sharable workflows and mappings, views of RDA content by table of contents and by element set, and links to other relevant cataloging resources.

Cataloging Correctly for Kids: An Introduction to the Tools, Fifth Edition: Based on guidelines issued by the Association for Library Cataloging and Technical Services (ALCTS), this handbook is a one-stop resource for librarians who organize information for children. Revisions include comprehensive updates on bibliographic description and subject access, new chapter exploring cataloging for non-English-speaking and preliterate children, and guidance on when and how to move to RDA, the next generation of cataloging guidelines.

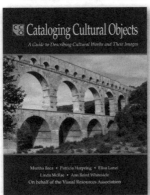

Cataloging Cultural Objects: A Guide to Describing Cultural Works and Their Images: This is a must-have reference for museum professionals, visual resources curators, archivists, librarians and anyone who documents cultural objects (including architecture, paintings, sculpture, prints, manuscripts, photographs, visual media, performance art, archaeological sites, and artifacts) and their images.

Magic Search: Getting the Best Results from Your Catalog and Beyond: Rebecca S. Kornegay and Heidi E. Buchanan, experienced reference librarians, and Hildegard B. Morgan, an expert cataloger, present the 467 best-performing LCSH subdivisions that speak to the kinds of research questions librarians handle every day. This handy reference format and index offers a useful tool to keep for quick reference rather than a cumbersome tome to be read from cover to cover.

Order today at www.alastore.ala.org or 866-746-7252!

ALA Store purchases fund advocacy, awareness, and accreditation programs for library professionals worldwide.